The Branding of MTV

Will Internet Kill the Video Star?

The Branding of MTV

Will Internet Kill the Video Star?

Paul Temporal

WILEY

John Wiley & Sons (Asia) Pte. Ltd.

Other Wiley Editorial Offices

John Wiley & Sons, Inc., 111 River Street, Hoboken, NJ 07030, USA
John Wiley & Sons Ltd., The Atrium, Southern Gate, Chichester,
    West Sussex P019 8SQ, UK
John Wiley & Sons Canada, Ltd., 5353 Dundas Street West, Suite 400, Toronto, Ontario,
    M9B 6HB, Canada
John Wiley & Sons Australia, Ltd., 42 McDougall Street, Milton, Queensland 4064, Australia
Wiley-VCH, Boschstrasse 12, D-69469 Weinheim, Germany

Library of Congress Cataloging-in-Publication Data
ISBN: 978-0-470-82271-5

Typeset in 11 point, Rotis Serif by Hot Fusion
Printed in Singapore by Saik Wah Press Pte. Ltd.
10 9 8 7 6 5 4 3 2 1

CONTENTS

ACKNOWLEDGMENTS

It is not possible to write a book about a global corporate brand unless the author is allowed access to that brand's corporate records. I would like to take this opportunity to thank everyone (past and present) from Viacom Inc., MTV Networks, and associated companies who provided me with assistance and information during the course of writing this book. In particular, I am grateful to Frank Brown, Jessica Kam, Sasha Rafi, and Joice Toh.

As MTV is a brand in a state of continuous innovation and evolution, the research has also been continuous and evolutionary, not to mention exhausting at times.
I would therefore like to thank Mary Bepono, Melody Wong, Sue Ann Chew, and Alifah Mohamed for the considerable time and energy they spent on researching various topics addressed in the book.

Special thanks go to Nick Wallwork and Janis Soo, of John Wiley & Sons (Asia), for their support and encouragement during this endeavor, and to Robyn Flemming for being a most helpful and understanding editor.

MTV Shows
Music Videos Be on MTV
Downloads Artist Photos
Live Performances
Genres
m Previews
Shop MTV Shows
Europe Music Awards   MTV Shows Gossip   TV Show Photos
Video Remixer   Billboard Charts

PREFACE

This book is not so much a tribute to MTV, although it deserves such, but more an analysis of how the MTV brand has been built and has achieved elite global brand status.

Global brands don't just arrive by accident; they are built carefully and strategically to match the needs of their target markets, and to evolve with those target markets' constantly changing lifestyles, wants, needs, attitudes, opinions, and interests, among many other factors. In addition, global brands manage global differences. Many brands don't make it to global status, as they fail to take into account the local nuances of different countries and cultures.

MTV has managed to do all of these things with startling consistency, another attribute of great brands that stand the test of time, and this is what makes the brand so fascinating. What is more intriguing is that it has done all this during one of the most turbulent times ever experienced in consumer markets—particularly in Asia, where change is endemic.

MTV has without any doubt revolutionized the worlds of music and television for youth since its inception. MTV—or Music Television, as it is more properly known—has become a global icon unrivaled anywhere in the world of music entertainment. But times change, and MTV itself is now the subject of a new revolution in technology convergence that threatens its very existence and, most certainly, its future brand dominance.

In this book you will discover how the MTV brand has been built and managed over its life span, and the challenges it now faces.

Chapter 1 describes the opportunity that was grasped by MTV from the early 1980s, when television provided the ideal vehicle for youth to explore its most desired form of entertainment—music. Chapter 2 looks at MTV's status as a global brand, and at what global brands have in common with respect to brand equity and value.

In Chapter 3, we analyze branding in the "Relationship Age," and look at how this impacts on youth. Chapter 4 discusses how MTV has responded to the changing nature of youth needs and wants over the past two decades. The focus is very much on the universal needs and wants of youth, and on what it takes to build a youth brand.

Chapter 5 homes in on the anatomy of the MTV brand—its ideation, vision, mission, and values—and discusses how these values have become a central part of the lives of youth today. Chapter 6 takes this analysis a step further and examines how the MTV brand has developed through various key business strategies and brand extensions, including how it has been managed through its program content, personality, global–local relevance, and co-branding and other initiatives.

Chapter 7 is focused on competitive analysis, and demonstrates just how far MTV has gone in outpacing the opposition. Chapter 8 links to this by closely following how brand execution has kept MTV at the forefront of change and brand evolution in line with the changing lifestyles of youth. Chapter 9 describes how the MTV brand is managed. Brand management is a complex business, and MTV seems to have good results in this area despite having little apparent formalized structure for this process.

Chapter 10 illustrates how MTV is responding to the development of two massive countries that contain one-third of the world's population and a greater percentage of the world's youth population—India and China.

Chapter 11 is in many ways the most intriguing chapter. While the book so far has described how the giant MTV brand has been built and managed, this final chapter looks at the challenges that now face the brand—in particular, those posed by the digital age. At its birth, the MTV brand took advantage of technology to link its offering with its target audience. However, technology has undergone massive changes in recent years, and its convergence has led to the delivery of entertainment through alternative channels—especially, the Internet. As television fails to interest youth in the ways it formerly did, this chapter looks at how MTV is responding to the new technology convergence revolution and asks whether it is adapting fast enough to maintain its global status going forward.

Writing this book has been an enormous task, made more challenging by the need to keep up with the relentless pace of change and innovation, both in the marketplace and within the MTV brand. As at mid-2007, the information contained here should be largely correct, but some facts may have changed since that time.

In analyzing how MTV has developed its iconic status, I have learnt much about the hard work and professionalism that goes into creating, developing, and managing a truly great and global brand. I hope that by reading this book, you will too. So, read on...

Paul Temporal

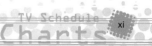

MTV Shows Music Videos Be on MTV
Live Performances Downloads Artist Photos
Shop MTV Shows Genres
Europe Music Awards MTV Shows Gossip Show Photos
Video Shop Charts
mtv

I

The Birth of MTV

There are certain times in people's lives when creative disruption occurs in a particular area and changes everything to do with that area and how it affects them. This is what MTV did in the early 1980s for the lives of youth around the world. Up until that time, for three decades, radio had ruled as the cheapest and most available source of music. By the late 1970s, however, it had become conservative and resistant to new music and new bands. The need to maintain current audiences to ensure advertising revenue had seen the industry stagnate. Youth demographics and psychographics were changing, but the very music industry that stood for the rock 'n' roll revolution was in danger of becoming mainstream.

Into this void swept MTV, or Music Television, which gave radio a face. Television had featured music videos before, but never had a whole new channel been devoted to them. Young people finally had a branded offering with which to identify themselves.

On August 1, 1981, at 12.01 a.m., (MTV was launched by then chief operating officer John Lack with the announcement:) "Ladies and gentlemen, rock and roll!" Music videos have since taken the world by storm, and it may not have been a coincidence that the first featured video was The Buggles' "Video Killed the Radio Star." It is true to say that, since those famous words were uttered, the music and television industries have never been the same. The convergence of these two mediums has been explosive in reaching out to young people the world over. MTV was custom-made for a generation, raised on television, that thrived on a pop culture, but which had no TV channel devoted to bringing the two together. MTV was the catalyst that brought rock music artists to a mainstream audience via television. Above all, it was a channel that enabled new artists to gain instant exposure through repeated airplay. As a result, radio soon began to play a secondary role to MTV in the delivery of the music experience.

Tom Freston, former Viacom co-president and chairman of MTV Networks, would later describe how television had never really had brands before—people watched programs, rather than channels. MTV's format was borrowed from radio, with videos taking the role of records. Its challenge was to create a sense of cohesion, a flowing link between the videos, so that the audience would identify with the channel and stay with it. And this is exactly what MTV did.

THE NEW BUSINESS OF MUSIC VIDEOS

Music videos were first made in the early 1980s in Europe as a medium for bands to promote themselves. At about the same time, they were starting to be screened in New York clubs. MTV realized the business potential of the format. Mike Nesmith, a former member of the 1960s' band The Monkees, was one of the inspirations for the channel. John Lack and a small group of enthusiasts at Warner-

Amex Satellite Entertainment Company (WASEC), a joint cable TV venture between Warner Communications and American Express, approached Nesmith and asked him to make a test version of MTV, which was shown on the children's channel Nickelodeon. Nesmith's involvement was short-lived, however; he was reluctant, he said, to be involved in "a channel full of commercials for records." Lack, on the other hand, believed that music television had a future like a marriage made in heaven. He persuaded WASEC's owners that the channel would be cheap to run, with music videos being provided by the promotional arms of the record labels. Lack was convinced that a music channel would be a winner.

The real challenge, however, was to sell the idea to cable operators, most of whom were unable to see the need for a music television channel. MTV responded with its "I want my MTV" advertising blitz. Featuring blockbuster videos by Duran Duran, Madonna, and Michael Jackson in its programming format, MTV appealed instantly to teenagers, who decided they all wanted their MTV. Faced with this sudden audience demand, cable operators had little choice but to carry the channel.

Artists who wanted their videos to be shown on MTV were soon pressuring their record companies, who were initially hesitant to provide the channel with free content. Ironically, MTV would rescue the record industry from the slump that had followed the era of "disco" music. By 1981, sales had slipped 30% from the industry's peak year of 1978. But with the presence of MTV, over the next decade sales soared. As the national sales figures rose, record labels began commissioning videos specifically for MTV, to promote new groups who were not touring or getting radio space. At the end of MTV's first year of operation, *Fortune* magazine declared it the "Product of the Year." MTV itself would go on to make the careers of hundreds of music acts, and would have a greater impact on the 1980s, and beyond, than any single artist.

FORGING THE MTV BRAND

The whole concept of the MTV brand revolved around youth. Record labels aside, no one had ever attempted to capture the elusive teenage market. MTV capitalized on the opportunities the concept presented: MTV appealed to teenagers, who felt it belonged to them. It was all about *their* music and culture; not their parents' or teachers'. This phenomenal market segment came to be known as the "MTV Generation." It was all about *seeing* music as well as listening to it, as the original slogan—"You'll never look at music the same way again"—cleverly declared. The unstructured format, with videos averaging just three to five minutes in length, was ideal for channel surfing. It required no commitment by the viewer: just like radio, MTV was meant to be left on all day as background to other activities.

The first images broadcast by MTV to accompany John Lack's announcement—including some doctored footage from the 1969 Apollo 11 moon landing that showed astronaut Neil Armstrong planting a flag bearing the MTV logo—signaled that MTV had arrived. (As the moon landing footage was considered to be firmly in the public domain, there was no copyright infringement.) Interestingly, rather than show something slick and corporate-like, that was out of touch with youth culture, the logo had a cartoon-like, graffiti appearance with which young people could identify.

Another significant brand feature of MTV, and first staged in September 1984 at Radio City Music Hall in New York, was its annual MTV Video Music Awards, or "VMAs." This glitzy affair, featuring the who's who of the music industry, was intended to be an alternative to the Grammy Awards. The award statues depicted "Moon Men," in apparent reference to the earliest representation of the MTV brand. Featuring Madonna's "Like a Virgin," Michael Jackson's "Thriller," and Eurythmics' "Sweet Dreams," the first awards show was typical MTV—brash and in-your-face—but it stamped its authority as a force to be reckoned with in the music industry. The yearly affair would become a brand in itself, so that 20 years on it now has representations in Europe, Asia, and Latin America. Viewers choose the award winners, reinforcing the channel's philosophy that MTV belongs to its audience.

In 1992, MTV would introduce its successful movie award show. These activities—and more that you will encounter later in this book—are typical of how MTV has demonstrated the essence of its brand, and how close it has been to understanding youth culture.

MTV GROWS UP

MTV was born in the USA, but it is now acknowledged as the leading global youth brand. As of May 2005, MTV was available through 56 channels to 495.2 million households in 179 countries/territories and in 27 languages.[1]

MTV's first international channel, MTV Europe, was launched on August 1, 1987. It was the start of MTV's global–local trend. While retaining its international flavor, it was decided to customize the channel so as to cater to the diverse tastes of audiences in different European countries, where MTV also had to compete with national and regional channels. The first video shown on the MTV Europe channel was the highly successful "Money for Nothing," by Dire Straits, which starts and finishes with the line "I want my MTV," sung by Sting.

To create brand awareness, MTV began sponsoring home-grown artists and events, as well as promoting tours of global superstars in Europe. It exported its brand ambassador, the MTV Video Music Awards event, and localized it as the MTV Europe Music Awards to make it more relevant to European audiences. With the advent of digital technology, MTV was able to broadcast to individual countries, featuring local artists and VJs (video jockeys—a play on the title "disc jockeys," who were presenters from radio) who spoke the local language, as well as regular MTV programming featuring international stars. The MTV brand is distinct in that it can provide creative and edgy programming while having a wide array of international artists at its disposal.

The conquest of Europe began in Germany, in 1997, and saw MTV Central, MTV's German-language service, taking on VIVA, a local German music channel that has since been acquired by MTV.

The United Kingdom and Ireland, Italy, Scandinavia, Spain, France, the Netherlands, Poland, Romania, and Portugal soon followed. MTV has also expanded its global–local channels throughout Asia, Australia, Canada, Latin America, Russia, and Africa.

MTV's strategy of reflecting the local youth culture and lifestyle, and of giving international exposure to local artists, especially in markets with their own indigenous pop cultures (such as Cantopop in Hong Kong and Bollywood in India), has won the hearts of its audiences the world over. In paternalistic Asian countries where youth culture and an indigenous-culture-based, grass-roots entertainment industry are discouraged, MTV fills the void. In addition to creating awareness of global superstars among local youth, it also promotes local talent and youth icons in its programming and reflects local cultural practices. For instance, MTV Indonesia includes a regular call to prayer for its Islamic audience, MTV Japan is very tech-oriented, and food programming is incorporated into the stylistic MTV Italy.

The heart of the MTV brand is its youthful take on the world and its ability constantly to evolve. These brand values translate into drivers that keep the staff inherently youthful, with a bottom-up culture that encourages the free flow of ideas and creates a fun place to work. MTV has established itself as *the* global youth brand.

MTV'S CURRENT GLOBAL STATUS

MTV's commanding status derives from its power to break and make artists simply by rotating their videos on air. It has changed the world's views on music and musicians. If an artist isn't featured on MTV, their career will be short-lived. Fledgling solo acts such as Marion Raven, formerly of the group M2M, have been fast-tracked to fame through MTV giving them constant airplay and promoting their events. Record labels looking for new acts monitor the singles featured on MTV in the hope of creating new markets and increasing sales. As such, there is no mistaking that the MTV phenomenon is a powerful business enterprise.

MTV's 100th channel—MTV Base in Africa—was announced in November 2004 by Judy McGrath, then CEO, now chairman and CEO of MTV Networks. McGrath described how, with more than 75% of MTV's channels based outside of the United States, it had become a truly global operation that is fueled by the exchange of creative ideas and cultures. There was no media company better positioned to benefit in the expanding international marketplace, she said.

Original content coupled with a "cool" image and independent attitudes have been the points of difference that have positioned MTV as a market leader in the crowded broadcast industry. The ability to react quickly is crucial when steering an operation the size of MTV. The inclusion of original local content that connects with local audiences helps to decentralize the business while maintaining the core brand values, which are essentially Western. This dichotomy of cultures around the core brand is a key factor in MTV's success. Tom Freston described the channel's business as being one of creative vision, smart brand building, unrelenting consumer focus, and good execution.

MTV also leverages its global status and influence through its corporate social responsibility (CSR) efforts and initiatives. MTV has a long history of promoting activism in young people with voting initiatives such as "Choose or Lose," and annual campaigns such as "Fight For Your Rights." *think* MTV, with its credo of "Reflect. Decide. Do." is another example of MTV helping young people to become informed and connected to each other, and to express themselves and take action on issues that are important to them, their community, and their world. *think* MTV joins with a large number of worldwide organizations, so enabling youth to become involved in important domestic and global issues of concern, such as sexual health, racial discrimination, the environment, and politics. Its format includes documentaries, international announcements, news segments, *think* moments, a comprehensive website (http://think.mtv.com), various media platforms, and grass-roots activities, materials, and issue guides.[2]

Even in the relatively conservative countries of Asia, MTV is giving young people a voice and a forum in which to discuss and raise awareness of issues such as HIV/AIDS, education, and poverty. In September 2005, MTV chronicled a visit to Kenya by the celebrity and social activist Angelina Jolie in a bid to highlight the plight of the nation's people. Jolie's visit was part of a United Nations effort to improve the standard of living in developing nations. MTV's status as a global media mogul enables it to give such initiatives unparalleled media coverage.

MUSIC: A UNIVERSAL PRODUCT AND LANGUAGE

The persuasive power of music has been recognized by thinkers as far back as Plato. Throughout history, rulers, bards, philosophers, and religious leaders have employed music and song to disseminate ideas, forge attitudes, and shape behaviors. The emotions expressed through music—especially about love and relationships—are a powerful means of gaining people's attention and motivating them to action. In fact, studies by neuroscientists have verified the powerful role that emotions play in our decision-making, so that things associated with strong memories are a powerful emotional trigger. It is no coincidence, then, that love songs often become chartbusters.

Elvis Presley was one of the first musical icons to converge African-American rhythm and blues with mainstream Western music. The resulting musical style, dubbed "rock 'n' roll," took the world by storm. Presley's sexually charged performances generated powerful, earthy emotions in his young audiences and raised the ire of their parents. For the first time, the commercial possibilities of popular music were recognized, paving the way for music to be promoted as a brand aimed at the young.

In the early 1960s, British bands such as The Beatles were pioneers in taking pop music to the world. They attained universal stardom on an unprecedented scale and opened the door for the many millionaire pop stars, with huge worldwide teenage fan followings, that came after. Popular music has become a universal product and a language shared by young people across the globe. It has surmounted differences of language and culture, and helped teens of all nationalities forge a sense of common identity. Today's contemporary pop has taken on a vast array of localized forms, whereby artists all over the world write and perform songs in hundreds of languages based on this genre of music.

The essence of music is that it is an easily acceptable mode of delivering a message. It triggers a response by penetrating through to the emotions. For this reason, music is a powerful branding tool, especially for the youth market.

SIAMESE TWINS: MUSIC AND YOUTH—INDEPENDENT YET INSEPARABLE

The saying "If music be the food of life, play on" sums up why music and youth are inseparable. The struggles of growing-up and having a taste of adult life present a world of uncertainties to youth everywhere. Many are experimenting with their identities and looking to express themselves on their own terms. Music fills the void as a channel of self-expression, giving it a key role in a young person's life. The anti-war, flower-power generation of the 1960s used songs to express their discontent about social injustices, as well as the need to "make love, not war." History is full of examples of bards who have been the voice of expression, and the social conscience, of their society.

Today's generation is no different, making music a lucrative expression of the youthful energy and aspirations of young people with short attention spans. Technological advances have enabled music to connect youth all over the world, giving them a sense of community. Forget about traditional record stores; Napster's downloads and Apple's iPods are the preferred music selection choice for the young. Fans of all musical genres the world over can chat, exchange information and reviews, and even view video clips online with one another.

Nowhere is the diversity of youth more clearly reflected than in the music business. The musical tastes of youth are also usually reflective of their brand preferences. Marketers wanting to tap this colossal market have always used music and popular artists to get across their message. Pepsi engaged Michael Jackson during the height of the "Thriller" phenomenon in the 1980s; later, Britney Spears' music video-like commercials helped make Pepsi the brand of choice of young people.

Contemporary pop music has become a universal voice for the young, and the young-at-heart, because it echoes their shared emotions, experiences, and aspirations—wherever in the world they live. MTV plays a major role in connecting the young to their world music. As an experiential channel, it gives them a sense of ownership, making it the perfect tool for delivering an attitude and a mindset. When viewers get to experience their genre of music on MTV, it creates an emotional link and builds relevance for the brand. Adding to this is the visual format: the emotions are conveyed directly from the "idol" to the viewer, making the MTV brand even more meaningful. As the standard-bearer for music, MTV has been able to transcend cultural borders and influence the behavior, and reflect the opinions, of young people worldwide. "Eighteen-year-olds in Paris have more in common with 18-year-olds in New York than with their own parents. They ... listen to the same music...," Bill Roedy, president of MTV Networks International, has said.

The "forever young" appeal of music is the secret to MTV's fountain-of-youth model. Every generation has had its fads, and MTV's ability to keep abreast of these has helped preserve its image of being young, cool, and hip. The brand is kept fresh through maverick genius programs such as *Fresh Produce*, featured on mtvU, which encourages viewers to send in personal video clips, including their own music recordings. This ideal viral marketing tool creates a two-way relationship with the audience: it gives them a voice, and possibly a break in the industry, while helping MTV stay in touch with viewer trends. With the advent of many other Internet players such as YouTube, Facebook, and MySpace, you will read more about the challenge to, and response of, MTV to changing youth media communications trends in the final chapter of this book.

Essentially, the MTV brand stays relevant to young people because it delivers a total music experience while remaining young by changing with the times. MTV's innovativeness is attributed to its always being in the know about youth trends, attitudes, and concerns. This interactivity helps MTV customize the brand to suit the tastes of its audiences, giving them a sense of being respected. This connectivity also keeps the brand fresh through the discovery of new talents. (For instance, the Russian girl duo Tatu was propelled to international stardom through worldwide exposure on MTV.) The connectivity strategy extends to MTV's VJ hunts in Asia, where the VJs are out on the streets meeting and relating to young people from all walks of life, in the search for new VJ talent.

The emotional triggers of musical connection, creativity, and a "cool" attitude have given MTV a powerful global youth culture mindset. MTV takes entertainment and music seriously. Its mission is to empower youth through interactive programs such as *MTV's Most Wanted* and *Total Request Live (TRL)*, and through having viewers vote for the winners of MTV's Video Music Awards. These viewers, known as the "VMA Nation," comprise a borderless marketplace populated by 94 million young, opinionated, and highly influential consumers. MTV is totally committed to connecting with this audience in a way that fuels their passion for music.

The huge popularity and longevity of the MTV brand can be ascribed to one thing: it embraces every individual, and offers them the ability to express their unique set of personality, attitudes, aspirations, and feelings. Simply put, if you are young or young-at-heart, the MTV brand is you—it represents who you are and whatever you want to be. It understands you and gives you a voice in the world.

In the next chapter, we will look at MTV's status as a global brand, and consider what it takes to achieve this elite status. In Chapter 3, we will delve further into branding in the "Relationship Age," and look at how this impacts on youth.

---

[1] MTV Networks International Global Fact Sheet, December 5, 2006.
[2] *think* MTV, http://think.mtv.com.

MTV Shows · Music Videos · Be on MTV · Live Performances · Downloads · Artist Hype · Genres · Shop MTV Shows · Europe Music Awards · MTV Shows Gossip · Show Photos · Videos · Shop · Stars

mtv

2

Building Global Brand Equity

INTRODUCTION

Few brands have made such a massive impact on the world stage in such a relatively short time frame as MTV. Today, MTV is a household name: most young people, regardless of whether they have access to television, have heard of it. It is a name associated with youth and music, and all that they stand for. MTV has dominated market space in the category of music television since its inception and looks as though it will continue to do so.

The ubiquity of its presence makes MTV a truly global brand, but this elite status isn't easily achieved. Indeed, many companies have had the ambition to become a global brand but have failed to do so. This chapter looks at global branding, and at what it takes to become a global brand.

CREATING A GLOBAL BRAND

True global brands are relatively few in number. What is a global brand, and how does it differ from an international brand? Most people would reply, if asked, that a global brand is one that has world market coverage and, to a certain extent, they would be correct. Taking Coca-Cola and McDonald's as two prime examples, there are few countries in the world that these two brands have yet to enter. So, in a sense, a global brand is one that is present in most markets in the world. Some writers say a rule of thumb for a global brand is to have a presence in over 100 countries.

Global brands have universal appeal and presence, not only in their names, but with their product offering as well. In order to satisfy these criteria, they have to be targeted at, and accepted by, global consumer segments.

Giant global brands aim for universal segments and gain a grip on certain types of customers. Demographically, there are many global segments: young people defined by certain age groupings, young mothers, young professionals, the gray segment of older and retired people, business travelers, and others. The people within each of these segments tend to share similar needs, wants, interests, lifestyles, aspirations, and attitudes. Only companies that understand what these psychographic features are, and who accordingly develop an idea that leads to products and services acceptable to the segment characteristics, can be successful in creating a global brand.

MTV's target customer base was originally identified as people aged 15 to 34 years, which might seem to be an enormous spread of the world's population. Indeed, a legitimate question is: how does MTV manage to satisfy the needs and wants of such a diverse audience? The answer is that, like all global brands, it does so by

understanding what goes on in the minds of its customers, not just demographically, but also psychographically with respect to attitudes, opinions, interests, and lifestyles, and by adapting the brand to each country in which it has a presence. Let's have a look at what this really means, starting with the global platform and its local adaptations.

GLOBAL–LOCAL BRAND ADAPTATIONS

Many of the top global brands of decades ago, such as Colgate, still enjoy the same ranking today and are showing no signs of terminal failure. In fact, it is important to note that, unlike products, brands don't have life cycles; if well looked after, they can achieve immortality.

But the longevity of global brands is no accident. Brand life can be extended by retaining the original strategic character and proposition of the brand while undertaking constant tactical innovation in product development and brand communications.

When a company is intent on building a global brand, it has to face up to the issue of to what extent it will attempt to project its values across all markets, and to what extent it will adapt these values to cater for different markets. There is no one right answer to this question of global versus local stances. Three main options are available.

Retaining the Same Basic Brand Personality and Proposition

A brand may have its own values and attempt to leverage these across all markets regardless of culture. This can work when there is an overriding area of universal emotional appeal, an example of which is the Nike brand with its focus on winning and empowerment.

Global brands that take this option generally stick to the same basic brand personality and proposition across the globe, while possibly adapting product and communications strategies to cater to the nuances of different cultures. The Body Shop, for example, doesn't alter its proposition of defending the environment and the creatures in it, despite modifying its product range from country to country.

Some global–local adaptations even take on local names, although the branded product remains the same. Coca-Cola, for example, changes its name to suit local cultures. Coca-Cola entered the Chinese market with the name (literally spelt) "kou-ke-kou-la." Unfortunately, in Chinese this meant (depending on the translation) "a thirsty mouth and full of candle wax" or "bite the wax tadpole." The Chinese name was subsequently changed to "ke-kou-ke-le," meaning "a joyful taste and happiness" or "happiness in the mouth." This change provided Coca-Cola with yet another resounding success story.

Combining Global Brand Values with Local Adaptations

A second option is to mix global brand values with local adaptations. For example, McDonald's pays attention to local palates in Muslim nations by complying with their halal requirements. This approach is popular when a brand cannot be accepted everywhere as is, and where it must pay attention to local cultural nuances of relevance to its business if it is to gain permission from consumers to become a part of their lives.

Companies such as Nestlé and Unilever opt for partial or complete local adaptations of most of their products. For example, they have many different names for similar products, and change some of the ingredients in their products, depending on the country. Nescafé customizes the formulation of its coffee according to local taste profiles. Some countries with strong taste palates prefer a stronger blend of the brew, whereas others prefer a milder blend.

McDonald's is positioned the world over as a family restaurant providing fun and value-for-money meals, but its menu changes according to local cultural preferences; for example, its outlets in Russia don't offer the Samurai burger that is popular with its customers in some Asian countries. Hence, it appears that customization of the McDonald's brand hovers around the percentage of global–local content.

To achieve this, global brands must walk the fine line of developing a concept that infuses local values into the brand according to the location, without diluting the original generic and global brand proposition.

Consumers generally find that global brands are more meaningful if they have been adapted to take into account the sensitivities of local markets—much like seeing your local "Idol" on the global *Idol* stage. The sense of recognition that comes with this "local voice" produces powerful emotions that are unlikely to be stirred by standardized, universal global corporate cultures that are mostly Western in origin.

Local or Fully Adaptive Branding

The third option, local branding (sometimes referred to as "fully adaptive branding"), has benefits for corporations, too. The company embarking on local branding of its global brand has the freedom to develop brand names, visual elements, and associations for each specific audience, and to produce them locally. It can also take advantage of the fact that the brand is regarded as a local one. In this extreme case, the brand values are not global in nature, and even the brand names may not be consistent. Holding companies such as Dutch supermarket giant Ahold adopt this stance with brands like Hypernova in Europe and Stop & Shop in the United States, but such companies are global businesses, rather than global brands.

The argument for fully adaptive branding is that there is a danger in global brand building of superimposing standardized, global brand values regardless of the local culture, and thus of making value judgments, and employing stereotyping and ethnocentrism.

Implications of Fully Adaptive Branding

It is true to say that, unless companies are fully convinced that their values have universal emotional appeal, then they must take into account different world cultures and views. Even technology-based brands, which were thought to be universal in nature, are realizing the importance of local input to their success. Ethnographers have observed that the ways in which people adapt such brands to suit local lifestyles have produced valuable insights for innovations better adapted to local market conditions. For example, Intel is using its own ethnographers and anthropologists to look at ways in which future technology devices may be able to be shared. The reason for this is that, in Asia, they found that there is a very strong culture of sharing, unlike in the West. Another example comes from the brand Coach, which, through the process of gaining insight into its consumers, found that Japanese consumers like small, cute items; this led the brand to downsize its whole product range, a hugely successful move.

THE MTV OPTION: COMBINING GLOBAL BRAND VALUES WITH LOCAL ADAPTATIONS

MTV's success has derived from mixing global values with local cultural adaptations. In leaning toward localization (its programming is estimated to be around 70% local and 30% global, although this is difficult to quantify), MTV gives each country, in which it has a presence, a great deal of autonomy in brand execution.

The reason would appear to be as follows. Although there may be some similarities among cultures, such as a universal youth culture, the case for studying how culture impacts brand building in the "Relationship Age" of the 21st century has never been stronger. (This is explained in more detail in Chapter 3.)

The need to adopt an anthropological perspective at a collective level, especially in the context of eclectic Asian cultures, takes precedence over the traditional Western perspective of the psychological aspect based on an individual level. Most global corporations develop different strategies for different countries in order to gain local recognition. A degree of flexibility is required to mould the brand structure to suit local or regional adaptations.

To achieve competitive advantage on a global platform, key cultural and national elements need to be identified and incorporated into the strategic operations adopted for, and approaches taken toward, particular markets. MTV has accomplished this by a mix of programming autonomy and local personalities, combined with its understanding of global youth values and universal music and artists.

THE CHALLENGES OF BUILDING A TRULY GLOBAL BRAND

There are many challenges to overcome in building a global brand, and companies can fall into many traps. Here are a few of the issues that companies can face.

Country of Origin

One pertinent focus in citing the difficulties of building a truly global brand is this global–local dilemma. "Globalization" remains the force of standardization, whereas "local" signifies differentiation. Just as no individual shares the same thumbprint, conformity remains a utopian ideal. That which is deemed to be culture free is actually culture bound by its country of origin. Coca-Cola, Levi Strauss, McDonald's, and Marlboro may be some of the most highly recognizable global brands, yet—like MTV—they are undeniably perceived as being American in origin.

> 66
> The rhetorician need not know the truth about things; he has only to discover some way of persuading the ignorant that he has more knowledge than those who know.[1]
> 99

Despite producing many high-quality products, the main resistance from international audiences to Chinese-branded goods is the "Made in China" tag. Yet, people across the world have no resistance to buying a pair of Nike trainers with the same label. Country of origin can either help or hinder brand development.

Technology

Even technology that was considered applicable across the board isn't exempt from this paradox. While the appropriate technology exists in theory, it still requires the "soft" side of the technology, which is adapting it to local conditions and ensuring its local appropriateness and sustainability. This strengthens the case for the specific versus the general.

Lack of Cultural Understanding

Ethnocentrism, or the perception that the culture of the company's country of origin is superior to that of other countries, has long been the culprit of biased advertising. Marketers who try to impose the aspirations of their brand's original culture on another have failed to grasp the sense of humility and modesty of the collective societies, especially in Asia. The value systems of the inherent Western concept of individualism often collide with the East's collectivism. Language, thought patterns, intellectual styles, signs, symbols, body language, imagery, and even music play a large part in the global versus local stage.

Markets are essentially people, wherein lies the dilemma. Underestimating the local culture and viewpoint—leading to seller-centric preoccupations, whereby marketers concentrate more on what comes out of the organization's operations than on the value that can be created in the life of the buyer—has produced many global casualties. Kellogg's nearly joined their ranks when it attempted to introduce its corn flakes into India in the normal advertising manner, without realizing that the preference in India is for hot milk on breakfast cereals—thus producing soggy corn flakes. Kellogg's overcame the problem by introducing wheat and rice cereals for this local market.

> There's an art to refashioning products made in the U.S. to suit local tastes... The mistake a lot of multinationals have made is looking at the size of the middle class, until they discover to their horror that you have to do things differently. You need to reflect the local culture.[2]

If not detected and rectified, such seller-centric perceptions can lead to a marketing disaster. Developing cross-cultural skills is essential in striking a balance between managing a global brand and being relevant and appealing to local markets. As you will see as you read through the book, much of MTV's success has arisen because it has successfully struck that balance.

A number of other global market developments in recent decades have created both challenges and opportunities for brand managers when trying to achieve a global presence. Below we consider a few of the changes the MTV brand has had to cope with in its rapid rise to global status.

GLOBAL MARKET DEVELOPMENTS

The role of brand building and brand management has become increasingly complex and important as a result of changes in the way businesses view their customers. Here are a few of the more significant developments.

The Age of the Big Brands

The late 1980s saw the arrival of powerful brands that dominated their chosen markets, led by highly experienced brand managers. Not only has there been a tremendous demand for luxury brands since that time, but other brands such as Nike have risen to fame and become global players. The whole world has now become more brand-conscious, with many research studies claiming that children become aware of brands from as young as four years of age. Even in the less developed and underdeveloped countries, the big brands have a presence and are the focus of consumer attention at all age levels.

However, the fragmentation of markets has led brand management into the complex world of mass customization, and there has been a strong movement away from pure generic products manufactured to suit mass markets. Brand management has now turned its attention to customizing generic products to the needs of different market segments, in the process creating a proliferation of products available to consumers and tremendous profits for those companies that understand these complex markets correctly. Mobile phones are a prime example of this, with Samsung producing four times the number of mobile models that Nokia does, with its philosophy of "more is better."

The Realization of Brand Value

It is now widely acknowledged that brands, if created, developed, and managed well, can achieve spectacular financial results. If we look at the market capitalization of heavily branded companies versus unbranded companies in both the United States and the United Kingdom (that is, companies listed on the S&P and FTSE markets, respectively), we see that around 70% or more of the market capitalization of the branded companies isn't represented by their net asset value. This huge gap between branded companies' market capitalization and their net tangible assets is accounted for by their intangible assets, a significant part of which is the value of the brand itself. Other intangible items can include patents, customer lists, licenses, know-how, and major contracts. Brand names are often worth multiples of the value of the actual business. For example, the value of the MTV brand has been calculated at US$6,627 million.[3]

A strong corporate brand name brings with it additional financial strength which can be measured and used in many ways, including the following:

- *Mergers and acquisitions:* Brand valuation plays a major part in these undertakings. Potential acquirers of branded goods companies, and their investors and bankers, find comfort in the knowledge that the price being paid for a company can be substantiated by reference to the value of specific intangible as well as tangible assets being acquired.

- *External investor relations:* Some major companies make building a portfolio of world-class brands a central objective. Brand valuation can be used to provide hard numbers in what is often a soft argument.

- *Internal communications:* Brand valuation can help to explain performance and be used to motivate management. The use of internal royalty rates based on brand values can also make clear to a group of companies the value of the corporate assets they are being allowed to use.

- *Marketing budget allocation:* Brand valuation can assist in budgeting decisions, providing a more systematic basis for decision-making.

- *Internal marketing management:* Strategic use of brand valuation techniques allows senior management to compare the success of different brand strategies and the relative performance of particular marketing teams.

- *Balance sheet reporting:* In some parts of the world, acquired brands are now carried as intangible assets and amortized.

- *Licensing and franchising:* Accurate brand valuation allows a realistic set of charges to be created for the licensing and franchising of brand names.

- *Securitized borrowing:* Companies such as Disney and Levi Strauss have borrowed major sums against their brand names.

- *Litigation support:* Brand valuations have been used in legal cases to defend the brand value, such as in cases of illicit use of a brand name or of receivership.

- *Fair trading investigations:* Brand valuation has been used to explain to non-marketing audiences the role of brands, and the importance their value has for the companies that spend so much to acquire and maintain them.

- *Tax planning:* More and more companies are actively planning the most effective domicile for their brand portfolios with branded royalty streams in mind.

- *New product and market development assessment:* New business strategies can be modeled using brand valuation techniques to make judgments on, for example, best brand, best market extension, and best consumer segment.

Brand Value versus Brand Equity

There is a distinct difference between brand value and brand equity, although the two are often confused. When we talk about "brand value," we mean the actual financial worth of the brand. "Brand equity," on the other hand, is often used in referring to the descriptive aspects of a brand—whether symbols, properties, imagery, or consumer associations—and reflects the more subjective and intangible views of the brand as held by consumers. The term is somewhat misleading, as "equity" has a financial origin.

There are several dimensions of brand equity as opposed to brand value. Some of these key aspects of brand performance or strength are:

- *price premium*—the additional price that consumers will pay for the brand compared to other offers;

- *satisfaction/loyalty*—levels of satisfaction with the brand that help to determine loyalty and prevent price sensitivity;

- *perceived quality* of the brand relative to others;

- *leadership*—in terms of market leadership, connected to market share;

- *perceived value*—a value-for-money concept linked not just to tangible items such as quality, but also to intangible factors;

- *brand personality*—the characteristics of the brand that differentiate it from others;

- *mental associations*—trust being the most important;

- *brand awareness and recognition*—key measures of brand strength concerned with how well the brand is known in the market;

- *market share*—volume, and in some cases perceived positioning;

- *market price*—premiums enjoyed by the brand; and

- *distribution coverage*—including percentage share.

Interestingly, the list contains a mixture of what could be seen as drivers of both brand value and brand equity. There may be a difference in terminology, but there is a connection between the concepts of brand value and brand equity, as many of the components of brand equity are the drivers of brand value. Modern business techniques enable this mix of attitudinal, behavioral, and market elements to be measured via the use of brand scorecards, and this is increasingly the focus for those involved in brand management.

While we don't need to go into detail here about the methodologies involved in calculating brand equity and brand value, it is important to make the point that companies wishing to achieve spectacular rates of return on investment should be focused on building up the strength of their corporate brand name in their chosen markets. As we look more closely at the MTV brand, we will see the existence of a similar kind of mixture of the drivers essential for global success.

BRAND OWNERSHIP

The movement toward a focus on the relationship between the brand and consumers has forced managers to answer the question of who actually owns and builds brands. Until recently, many companies were of the view that *they* build brands. However, leading brand companies now acknowledge that it is the *consumer* who owns and builds brands. These enlightened companies know that brands exist only in the minds of consumers, and that without the psychological commitment from consumers, they are—and will remain—merely companies, products, and services. MTV really understands its customers, and in return its customers have built and "own" the brand.

The next section examines MTV's brand equity, which I believe is where its strengths lie.

MTV'S BRAND EQUITY

MTV is saleable because it has created an image for its advertisers that they know young people well. Young people connect with and feel a part of MTV, to the point that they are identified as the "MTV Generation" or "MTV Nation." MTV's strong brand equity allows for brand extensions with high success rates, such as mtvU, MTV2, and so on.

Key Aspects of MTV's Brand Performance

There are several dimensions of brand equity that relate to MTV. Some of the key aspects of brand performance, or strengths commonly measured by valuation and research companies, are discussed below.

Satisfaction/Loyalty

The determiners pertaining to loyalty and satisfaction revolve around MTV's relevance to its viewers. Its passionate, unpredictable, clever, humorous, risk-taking, bold, and open attitude reinforces the honest and realistic approach it takes to the viewer.

Perceived Quality

MTV's status as the leading voice of youth culture has even been acknowledged by the United Kingdom's, former prime minister, Tony Blair, who chose MTV as the platform for reaching out to young people in conjunction with the G8 summit in July 2005. The program, *All Eyes on Tony Blair*, was a live 60-minute forum that gave young people from the UK, and around the world, an opportunity to ask the prime minister incisive and provocative questions on Africa and climate change, the two main agenda items for the G8.

MTV's product content is of the highest quality. Despite the myriad of regions and cultures represented by its audience, MTV manages to differentiate itself from its competitors by appealing to, and staying relevant and in touch with, its viewers through its creative content, high-quality graphics, and attitudes that reflect the views of local audiences.

Leadership

MTV's vast corporate resources give it the status of first mover, market leader, and icon. This gives the channel market accessibility coupled with limited risk, as its success factors are achievable with limited budgets. When researching the market in Russia, MTV Networks International conducted a survey on perceptions of MTV in that country. Two versions of an archetypal program were shown to participants—one quite tame and the other considerably more outrageous. The majority of viewers preferred the wilder version. "It told me to never underestimate the willingness of the audience to embrace MTV," commented the company's president, Bill Roedy.

Perceived Value

By providing a multiplicity of genres that cater to varied musical tastes, MTV provides a sense of inclusion and belonging to young people—as well as to the young-at-heart—the world over. Non-music programming such as *Real World*, pioneers of reality TV, understood the need for self-expression among teenagers making the sometimes-difficult transition from childhood to adulthood. Viewers learnt about HIV/AIDS and other issues that were relevant and important to them. *The Osbournes*, a more realistic view of family life, was born out of young people's need in the West to identify with shifting parent–child relationships.

It is the flow of content, spoken in a language that young people all over the globe can identify with, that makes MTV a key proponent of youth culture in accordance with its vision and mission. MTV allows young people to be aware of current trends and "what everyone's talking about." The opportunity to interact via the Internet, text messaging, and fax gives viewers a voice. The excitement and fun experiences are further generated by viewer contests, discount concert tickets, and so on, which inspire viewers to "be a part of MTV."

Brand Personality

The personality's creative filters—relevance, passion, unpredictability, cleverness, humor, willingness to take risks, boldness, openness, and "no bullshit"—give MTV the opportunity to build the "differentiation" it needs. MTV treats its viewers as active and intelligent people who deserve to be respected. The inclusiveness of the brand inspires viewers to participate and revel in the musical experience. "We don't treat viewers like couch potatoes—in fact we inspire them to go and see a band, buy a CD, go to a movie... That's why it's a stamp of credibility for an artist to appear on MTV. We're not observing youth culture from on high—we are right at the heart of it," says Brent Hansen, formerly of MTV Networks Europe. MTV's wide distribution access and first-to-market status still make it the channel of the "Millennial Generation."

Brand Awareness and Recognition

MTV's first marketing slogan, the inclusive "I want my MTV," impressed on its young viewers that the channel was produced by like-minded people who understood their needs and aspirations. The driving force of MTV's brand loyalty has remained this sense of ownership, which is conveyed to viewers through celebrating today's music experience, providing a personal connection with young people, and expressing their attitudes, styles, and interests. "Sometimes I can't believe how truly global MTV has become, compared to how it started," said Bill Roedy. "I once met the [former] Chinese leader Jiang Zemin, and the first words out of his mouth were, 'Oh, MTV'. He knew exactly what the brand was all about."[4]

Distribution, Co-branding, and Alliances

Currently reaching millions of viewers throughout the world, MTV is the preferred choice of advertisers. MTV has been ranked the world's most valuable media brand for many years, and looks certain to continue in this position. "Media moguls can babble on about the global village, about how CNN or BBC can reach out and touch the world. But those news shows are bush league operations compared to MTV's clout."[5] Separate country feeds give brands the flexibility to tailor campaign buys by country. Up to 65% of MTV's programming is local in order to maximize local relevance while balancing global edge. This gives MTV's partners further flexibility and local market relevance when building their brands. MTV anchors the connection in a highly relevant and powerful environment where brands flourish when invention and innovation are the kinetic drivers of relevance. MTV's concierge-like role is the catalyst for youth, as it recognizes the smart consumer within its viewers. Hence, the channel's approach celebrates the intelligence of its viewers.

Sunil Lulla, former general manager of MTV India, once said: "There is an increasing set of evolved marketers, who—to address their market segment—need to talk, interact and have a dialogue with the consumers. MTV is good at making a connection with the viewers."[6]

By reaching out and understanding its viewers' needs and preferences—in effect, putting young people in charge—MTV stays relevant to its market. As a catalyst for youth, alliance partner marketers benefit from the aura of credibility generated by MTV. The channel reflects the image of the brand. Marketers can leverage its creative vision and expertise to deliver a unique and customized youth marketing strategy for their brands.

For example, when co-branded partnerships occur between sponsors/advertisers and MTV, MTV ensures that there are fully integrated 360-degree on-air, on-the-ground, online, licensing, merchandising, and joint press activities/marketing strategies to support and reflect the brands. Leong Han Kong, vice president of marketing with Imaging and Printing Group, HP Asia Pacific and Japan, said of Hewlett Packard's involvement as a sponsor for the MTV Asia Awards 2005 that MTV has the power to resonate with young Asians like no other brand. HP's sponsorship of the MTV Asia Awards has allowed the company to plug right into this pool of vibrant consumers. The sponsorship, Leong said, has helped refresh HP's brand relationship with young people.

Judging by MTV's current co-branding partners, it is obvious that the channel is on a different plane altogether to its competitors and has left them light years behind. The exclusive list includes Apple, Buena Vista Pictures, Caltex, Canon, Club Med, Nokia, McDonald's, and Hugo Boss, among other leading global brands.

MTV remains the preferred choice for co-branding partners who want to reach out to the "Millennial Generation." One such example is the Singapore-based United Overseas Bank's (UOB) MTV Card, in association with MasterCard, which "is targeted at those who desire their plastic to be more than just a credit card, what with its many privileges and access to the dazzling world of MTV events."[7] Peter Bullard, former senior vice president, MTV Asia and managing director, MTV Southeast Asia, said:

> ❝ MTV has become synonymous with all that's hip and youth-oriented. MTV's vision is to become the first-choice, music-based youth entertainment brand in Asia. We want to establish a personal connection with today's youth in every aspect of their lives and their lifestyles.[8] ❞

CONCLUSION

As we have seen, it is no easy task for any company to build a global brand. One of the biggest challenges faced is to generate a strong relationship between the brand and its customer group in many different markets. MTV has accomplished this by understanding what makes youth tick and giving them what they want, both in terms of universal desires and local relevance. As a result, it has gained huge brand equity and value.

In the following chapter, we will delve more into the world of youth, and discover what really drives this huge part of the world's population.

[1] Plato, Gorgias 380 BC, Part 2 – Translated by Benjamin Jowett
http://graduate.gradsch.uga.edu/archive/Plato/Gorgias.txt

[2] Alex Kuruvilla, quoted by Marc Gunther, "MTV's Passage to India," *Fortune*, August 9, 2004, p. 116.

[3] "The 100 Top Brands 2006," *BusinessWeek*, July 28, 2006, http://bwnt.businessweek.com.brand/2006/.

[4] Mark Tungate, *Media Monoliths: How Great Media Brands Thrive and Survive* (London: Kogan Page, 2004), p. 45.

[5] "MTV's World: Mando-Pop. Mexican Hip Hop. Russian Rap. It's all fueling the biggest global channel," *BusinessWeek,* February 18, 2002, http://www.businessweek.com/magazine/content/02_07/b3770009.htm.

[6] "Channel [V] vs MTV: It's Open War," http://www.screenindia.com/nov07/tele1.htm.

[7] United Overseas Bank, "MTV and UOB launch Southeast Asia's first MasterCard credit card for MTV fans in Singapore," http://www.uobgroup.com/pages/investor/news/newsreleases/2002/news_26sep02.html.

[8] Ibid.

3

21st-century Branding:

The "Relationship Age"

INTRODUCTION

In order to understand how a brand with the power of MTV relates to youth, we first have to understand how youth thinks; we have to develop what brand managers call "consumer insight." Many studies of youth culture and trends have been carried out, and a summary of current thought is given below, starting with mutualism and the "Relationship Age." The "Relationship Age" has had a profound impact on how global brands have changed their ways of relating to consumers, and MTV has also moved with the times.

33

MUTUALISM: BRANDING IN THE "RELATIONSHIP AGE"

The "Relationship Age," with all the complexities of the new millennium and its uncertainties, has replaced the certainties of the second half of the 20th century, known as the "Transaction Age." Mutualism, or the search for the noble human spirit through the channel of relationships, is the compelling force of the "Relationship Age." Organizations need to embrace these mutually dependent human traits of engagement, empathy, and trust if they are to succeed in this new era. Businesses must understand the needs both of individuals and society, as well as their interdependency; and therein lies the challenge of dethroning the organization and ensuring the rise of the humanistic, values-oriented new economy.

Gone are the hedonistic days of the "Me Generation" and false consumer consciousness. What organizations now need to hear loud and clear is: "It's truthfully about us." The nuances of the "Relationship Age" demand that corporate responsibility means more than simply building shareholder value by any means possible. This revolution of people power has been achieved at a

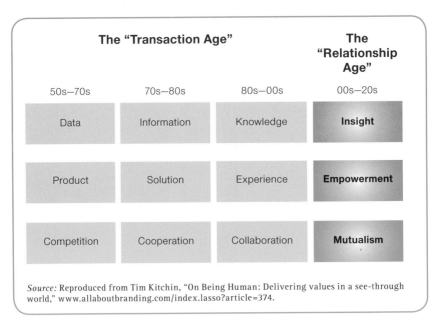

The "Transaction Age"			The "Relationship Age"
50s–70s	70s–80s	80s–00s	00s–20s
Data	Information	Knowledge	**Insight**
Product	Solution	Experience	**Empowerment**
Competition	Cooperation	Collaboration	**Mutualism**

Source: Reproduced from Tim Kitchin, "On Being Human: Delivering values in a see-through world," www.allaboutbranding.com/index.lasso?article=374.

Figure 3.1 The "Relationship Age"

great price, causing the very young to grow up at an accelerated pace. Figure 3.1 illustrates the important shifts that have occurred in corporate–consumer relationships since the 1950s, which are described briefly below:

- *From Information* ➤➤ *Insight*
  Information no longer remains an external tool, but is used to develop consumer *Insight* that becomes a catalyst for change.

- *From Content* ➤➤ *Connection*
  The insights gleaned from the *Content*, when internalized, lead to a much closer and empathetic *Connection* with the consumer.

- *From Understanding* ➤➤ *Learning*
  Moving on from just *Understanding* consumers serves to expand the *Learning* curve that could further enhance corporate behaviors as well as brand development.

- *From Participation* ➤➤ *Support*
  Mere *Participation* turns to interaction with consumers and is perceived by them as genuine *Support*, which they reciprocate.

- *From Fact* ➤➤ *Opinion*
  Companies no longer take in *Facts* and use them rationally, but turn them into *Opinions* that further strengthen emotional connections with consumers.

- *From Personality* ➤➤ *Character*
  Positive opinions transform the passive brand *Personality* into a responsible, strong, and active *Character*.

The "Relationship Age" reinvents the corporate–consumer relationship, giving power to the consumer. But what are the implications of this for brands?

FUNCTIONAL AND EXPERIENTIAL BRANDS: ONE SIZE DOESN'T FIT ALL

The branding or re-branding cycle has been differentiated for today's market. We are in the age of globalization, and yet forces against globalization are in evidence everywhere. The "Relationship Age" has decentralized businesses—formerly the power base of the "Transaction Age"—as the focal point. The new determinants of competitive strategies for organizations are individuals, and how they create value for one another.

Relationships are fostered through real experiences, dialogue, transparency, and accountability. This is achieved through community-building initiatives whereby organizations reach out and understand the inherent market differences that exist around them. Obviously, one size doesn't fit all. For example, current consumer trends suggest that there is inherent advertising fatigue, where 20th-century branding has a negative effect—especially on young people. We live now in the age of mass customization, not mass marketing.

Localization is an example of the trend in the "Relationship Age" for organizations to realize the inherent market differences that exist from country to country, and to cater for groups of individuals. For instance, corporations such as Unilever had to contend with the strong spiritual beliefs and national character of the halal Muslim Asian markets that were able to be capitalized on by local brands. Organizations today are acutely aware that there can never be a single sweeping plan to deal with disparate cultural issues and behaviors, occurring more or less at the same time around the world. The secret is to analyze these diversities and draw meaningful conclusions to be used as vital and actionable market feedback. MTV appears to do this effortlessly, although in reality it does so through a combination of hard work and skill, as you will see throughout this book.

CHANGING CONSUMER PREFERENCES IN AN EVOLVING CULTURAL LANDSCAPE: PRAGMATIC ETHICS AND CONTINUOUS IMPROVEMENT

The prominent group of consumers at present is the Millennial Generation, sometimes called "Generation Y" or "The Millennials"– those born since 1982. Essentially, these consumers follow on from their predecessors, known as "Generation X." (MTV addresses both audiences, Gen Y through its normal channel MTV and Gen X through its brand extension VH1–as well as younger viewers through Nickelodeon–see Chapter 6.

The Millennials' access to knowledge and information is unparalleled by any other generation and will most likely shake the world and its establishments. Studies reveal that this age group, because they are the most informed, will insist on solutions being found to society's problems and injustices. They are more spiritually attuned, willing to uphold basic human rights and to fight against racism and oppression, as well as being environmentally conscious. Issues surrounding genetic engineering and biotechnology, economic fairness in an emerging global economy, and closing the digital divide play a vital role in the borderless world of the Millennial Generation.

A keen awareness that their choices of today will surely affect their lives tomorrow permeates this generation more than any previous one. The Millennials possess a sense of civic virtue and understand the need for a pragmatic code of ethics. The information overload within this generation has made them realize that the basis· for conflict resolution lies in tolerance and the acceptance of people different from themselves. They understand both the consequences of their own actions and the effects of their actions on others.

The demand will continue to grow for organizations to build on ethical behavior and civic responsibility. Paramount in this are community-building concepts such as courtesy, due process, honesty, integrity, justice, respecting the rights of others, tolerance, and truth. Thus, Millennials tend to focus on family, religion, and community issues, and gravitate away from the extreme rebelliousness we saw with previous generations. The trend patterns of the Millennial Generation include:

- smaller family units and warmer relationships between teenagers and their parents;

- an increasing parental obsession with the safety and education of children;

- a weakening of negative social trends among teens; and

- the widespread use of mobile phones and the Internet for peer-to-peer communication.

A good example of an organization's human face in the "Relationship Age" would be the highlighting of the plight of the African continent by the UK government during the 2005 G8 summit. Coincidently, London won the 2012 Olympics bid at about the same time as the city was portrayed as being very diverse, young, and vibrant.

Most Millennials have been saturated with brands from an early age, especially since television and the Internet have been a major part of their lives. It is a fact that children are now brand-conscious from around the age of four and have preferred brands firmly in their sights by the age of seven. Thus, it is not surprising that as they grow up they become very brand-savvy consumers who are avidly involved in a majority of the family's purchase decisions. This coming together of social responsibilities, international events, and technological developments within the Millennial Generation creates new opportunities for marketing success or failure. Competition, technology, new thinking, and a growing impatience among people who demand quality and effectiveness in products and services that meet their needs like never before, invigorate the thrust for continuous improvement.

Organizations are taking the need for continuous improvement seriously, by identifying problems and making improvements, as well as instituting system-wide reforms in order to stay in sync—rather than sink—in the "Relationship Age." At the heart of this change in attitude is the realization that companies need to build emotional capital in order to survive. This exemplifies a leadership style which accepts that no matter how good one is today, the uncertainties of tomorrow could produce a different story altogether.

BUILDING EMOTIONAL CAPITAL THROUGH THE CONVERGENCE OF IDEAS

The "Relationship Age" focus seeks to bring the customer's voice into brand and product development. Unlike traditional market research, which relies heavily on focus groups to understand how people respond to specific brand-related initiatives, the relationship imperative focuses on the context of individuals' lives, in order to understand their goals and ideas about their world.

The goal is to make a connection between the brand/company/product and consumers, to gain an in-depth view of how customers accomplish everyday tasks, and thus to provide a holistic view of their needs and wants. This convergence of ideas involves new ways of thinking out of the box, fueled by changing technology, demographics, and consumer habits. The emergence of the "consumer as king" is virtually undeniable, as customer involvement is inevitable for a brand's success. Traditionally, much lip service has been given to this statement, but in the 21st century, those who don't deliver on it won't survive. As the strategist and writer C. K. Prahalad says, "Today's customers are more informed, networked, active, and global. These new market characteristics have led to a new form of value creation, where value is co-created by both the company and its customers."[1]

Martin Lindstrom, who with Patricia B. Seybold, founder and CEO of Patricia Seybold Group, wrote *Brandchild*, explains why this is so financially important to businesses:

> This is a generation that spends in excess of US$150 billion a year. And if this is not enough, then add another US$150 billion because that's the amount that this generation actually controls when their parents are supposedly in the driver's seat, holding on to the family's purse strings. From a purely monetary perspective, it's no wonder that this generation has created such enormous attention and wielded so much influence among companies and their brands.[2]

But as every brand builder knows, connecting with youth means that a company has to achieve a strong emotional relationship. In order to build emotional capital among such consumers, marketers need to sell dreams, concepts, and aspirations, rather than products, as the hard sell no longer works with the pervading youth culture. CEO of the Gucci Group and former head of the Unilever frozen food and ice cream division, Robert Polet, explains: "I didn't sell ice cream. I sold concepts. I sold worlds in which people consume ice cream, but I didn't sell a piece of vanilla with a chocolate topping on a stick."[3]

The need to cement brand preferences from a young age cannot be over-emphasized. Young people are now becoming very brand-conscious, and even making their own choice of brands, from the age of seven or so. It's not unusual to find that they will form an attachment to these brands and possibly stay loyal to them over many years. Accomplishing this is another question altogether, especially among the worldly-wise Millennials. The forging of one's identity is dominant in the psyche of youth culture, which includes developing relationships with peers. Thus, friendships that create a sense of belonging are a vital part of young people's lives. Preferences for fashion, music, technology, and recreation revolve around how they perceive themselves in relation to their friends. These expressions of being part of the group are so crucial that to be non-conforming could spell social suicide. The convergence of practicality with the forging of identities and the fulfillment of dreams is the key to building emotional capital in young people.

Brand Building and Emotional Capital

As a result of the above-mentioned major changes in the world to which youth belongs today, brand building and management is increasingly pursuing an emotions-focused strategy in order to win and keep customers. In essence, a brand is a relationship, and that is precisely what today's consumers are looking for—brands that develop and grow relationships.

The power brands such as Nike develop emotional capital, for the following reasons:

- *They are very personal:* People choose brands for very personal reasons, including as a form of self-expression, to create a sense of belonging, etc.

- *They evoke emotions:* Brands can unleash unstoppable emotion, arousing passion and unquestionable excitement.

- *They live and evolve:* Brands are like people in that they live, grow, evolve, and mature. But luckily, if they are well managed, they have no life cycle and can live forever.

- *They communicate:* Strong brands listen, receive feedback, change their behavior as they learn, and speak differently to different people, depending on the situation, just as people do. They believe in dialogue, not monologue.

- *They inspire immense trust:* People trust the brands they choose, and often resist all substitutes.

- *They engender loyalty and friendship:* Trust paves the way for long-lasting relationships, and brands can be friends for life.

- *They give great experiences:* Like great people, great brands are nice to be with, good to have around, and are consistent in what they give to their friends.

Given these facts about the emotional capital that brands develop, we need now to move on to see how they actually do it. What is the process of establishing an emotional relationship with consumers?

Emotion Sells

Building relationships with consumers starts by making emotional connections with them. The onus is on companies, who have the responsibility to be receptive, to listen, and to relate to people. Ultimately, all brands aim for trust and loyalty from their consumers; once developed, this can lead to the elusive catch of lifetime customers.

P. Read Montague, a neuroscientist at Baylor College of Medicine in Houston, Texas, has demonstrated the power of emotions and their strong influence expressed through brand loyalty. Montague studied the power of emotions via the now famous Coca-Cola and Pepsi taste tests and recorded the responses using functional magnetic resonance imaging (fMRI) technology.

In the brand-cued experiment, brand knowledge for one of the drinks had a dramatic influence on the subjects' brand preferences, as well as on the measured brain responses on the fMRI scan. This was particularly so in the case of Coca-Cola, for which brand information significantly influenced the subjects' preferred choice. This simple observation strengthens the case for how emotions can help shape perceptions, even to the point of modifying preferences for a basic aerated—albeit popular—drink. The power of emotions, which is the intangible associated with the

Coca-Cola brand, is the key reason why Coca-Cola outsells Pepsi by 2:1, despite taste tests suggesting the opposite, and remains the world's most valuable brand.

Many companies are using brain-scanning techniques today to help understand how emotions are developed and displayed. They understand that people, and youth in particular, use brands as symbols in various ways.

Brands Are Now Emotional Symbols

The real essence of a brand is the values and associations that are wrapped around the basic product or service. The establishment of a brand personality brings these attachments to life by acting as symbols for the thoughts and fantasies of consumers who buy them. Brand personality, discussed in Chapter 5, can strengthen the brand–consumer relationship through the development of powerful emotional associations. These associations result from the pull of emotional appeal and can symbolize several things to people, including:

- what they stand for
- what they believe in
- what they care about
- what they love
- what they want to be
- the type of person they want to be with
- the kind of relationship they want
- what they want people to know about them
- the kind of friend they want.

In my book *Branding in Asia*,[4] I developed from my Asian research the following classification, which illustrates some of the inner needs and associations that most youth would want their brands to be and to express.

➤ *The loyal friend*

People sometimes feel lonely and need someone to talk to. Brands can become the kind of friend that fulfills this role. The brand a person always consumes can develop this relationship. Research can elicit these thoughts by asking consumers to describe positive feelings about the brands they use, examples of replies being:

"I miss you when you're not with me."

"I have lots of fun with you."

"I can't wait until we see each other again."

➤ *The cult of belonging*

Although every person is unique, each has the same need of wanting to be with others. We tend to have the need to belong or to associate ourselves with others, be it formally or informally, and Starbucks is a brand that fills this need. Brand personalities provide the impetus for role modeling and for becoming one of a special crowd. The Body Shop provides the opportunity to be active in saving the environment and protecting animals; and Nike allows young people to be part of the sports club of their choice and to be "friends" with their heroes. Youth yearns to belong.

➤ *The dream team*

Brands can take people to the dizzying heights of success that are the stuff of dreams. You can dress like the Hollywood stars, be part of the elite business community, or wear the same sports gear as Olympic athletes. Kids can become superstars, just like their heroes. Nothing seems impossible when you buy the right brand. The use of real personalities, such as golfer Tiger Woods, brings brands to life and helps make dreams come true. For youth, dreams, hopes, and aspirations occupy their minds and hearts to a large degree.

➤ *The real me*

From aspiration to revelation, brands can reveal the real you if you want them to. Brand choices reveal lifestyles, hopes, interests, and successes, and provide the opportunity for every person to express his or her own personality. The clothes you wear, the car you drive, the drinks you order, and the brands you buy paint a picture of the kind of person you are and the life you lead. Sometimes there is a difference between the "real me" as I normally am and the "real me" I want to be.

For example, at home I might just want to put on my favorite brand of jeans and T-shirt and relax, because I feel that is the homely me—feeling comfortable with my friendly clothes and myself. For a dinner or cocktail party, I might wear a really smart, or possibly even a stunning outfit, because I want people to see my sophisticated side. Brands are the vehicles that allow everyone to show others what they are and can be like. Brands can help you say, "Hey, this is me!" in a variety of ways.

The MTV brand offers all these associations for its target audience. It emotionally relates on different planes to various ages and personalities; and it climbs the emotional ladder of success that makes a brand great, a concept that is described below.

The Emotional Ladder of Brand Success

In order to build an emotional brand strategy there are certain steps brand managers need to take, like the steps of a ladder, as shown in Figure 3.2. Let's think of it as two people, as opposed to a brand and consumers. One person sees another across a room at a particular function, and wants to meet them. Following this awareness, an opportunity to meet may arise, and although the conversation is short, it does lead to the decision as to whether or not the interest is sufficient to carry the relationship further. Further meetings reinforce this mutual respect and the two people become friends. If the friendship blossoms, it generates trust and loyalty between them, and it is highly likely that they will have an enduring relationship and may even become friends for life.

The brand–consumer relationship grows in a very similar way. Awareness comes first, followed by involvement and purchase—

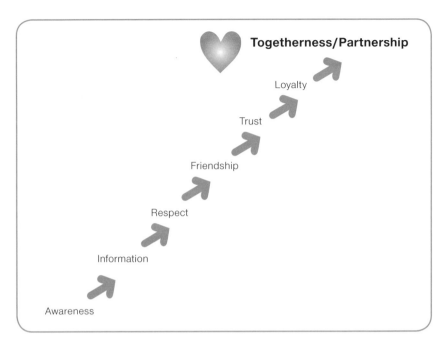

Figure 3.2 – The Emotional Brand Relationship Process

a few meetings—which can lead on to the friendship and trust levels, which in turn lead to brand loyalty and lifetime customer relationships. The power brands get to and past the friendship and trust levels; those that don't get that far can often get stuck at the first stage. In fact, big spending on awareness follows many brand launches, but the subsequent management of the brand may not take it up the ladder. Some companies spend millions on awareness—which is an essential step to achieve—but then neglect the emotional side of the brand–consumer relationship, which is necessary for real long-term success.

RELATIONSHIP DYNAMICS: CONTINUOUS IMPROVEMENT

Branding is the key to breaking out of the commodity trap. It transcends and transforms the organization's image by leveraging on subterranean emotional connections with consumers. The crux of this lies in "Continuous Improvement," whereby standards are raised to meet customer expectations, lending a greater sense of intent to the relationship. The worth of the relationship is usually reflected in the organization's qualitative intangible assets.

Nokia is an organization that thrives on "Continuous Improvement," and this sets it apart from its competitors. In the highly competitive industry of mobile technology, Nokia's network-focused and customer-driven downstream innovations have ensured its success. The mobile phone giant maintains its global market leadership not just through its consistent performance improvements and liberating innovations, but by its amazing ability to understand its customers and anticipate what they want next.

The successful businesses of today concentrate on getting close to the consumer, developing tremendous consumer insight, and thinking from the "outside-in," as opposed to the "inside-out"— that is, finding products to suit consumers, and not vice versa. Trends in world marketing are thus moving toward presenting a more human face for companies. As businesses come to understand consumers more, they have found that in the 21st century there is a massive appetite for empowerment.

The Search for Empowerment

More than ever before, people are looking for ways to allow them to do what they want, when they want to, with whom they want, and how they want. Youth is no different. To sum up what youth is looking for we can phrase a quotation as follows: "I am free to express my needs and wants; getting rid of unrealistic thinking and making room for spontaneity. I care about you enough to allow you to like and love me, which sets me free from repressed feelings, rigidity, and inflexibility. I am in a position where I can communicate exactly what I think and feel, freeing me to experience intimacy and fulfillment in my relationship."

These are the deep-seated emotional patterns underlying young people's behavior and reveal their need to feel empowered.

Empowered Consumers

The consumers of the "Relationship Age" want to participate in any dialogue that will allow them to be heard, hence the advent of Web "blogging" in the form of online chat rooms or forums where people from all over the world can have their say on issues of concern and interest. There is a great distrust of news broadcasts on television and radio, as most young people are suspicious of the "propaganda" perpetuated by the official news sources. Blogs give people opportunities to voice their opinions and listen to others, thus creating a grapevine that exists in an alternative, parallel world to that of officialdom.

Entertainment has taken on new dimensions with the advent of reality TV shows. The *Idol* series is hugely popular and has many local versions all over the world, with viewers voting for their favorite contestant via text messaging. This empowerment of the viewer has been devised to curb the channel-switching tendencies that the remote control encourages.

The need to capture the attention of viewers has never been more urgent, with consumers being bombarded with more than 5,000 messages a day via television, radio, cable and satellite channels, the Internet, and so on. These empowered, intelligent consumers, who have an unprecedented range of choice for products and services, demand a higher level of quality, integrity, and trust from corporations from all quarters in order to build brand loyalty among them.

Ethnography and Corporate Anthropology

Ethnography is the branch of anthropology that deals with the scientific description of specific human cultures and their link to behaviors. Ever since applied-anthropology legends Lucy Suchman and Julian Orr studied how people interacted with technology at Xerox's Palo Alto Research Center in the 1980s, many corporations have understood the value of using ethnographers. The practice has grown rapidly in recent years as corporations attempt to fine-tune consumer research by assessing products using ethnography.

Ethnographers live among communities to study people and issues that are important to them. They gather valuable information about consumers' lives, which is then relayed to corporations so that they can better relate to consumers and create products and services that are more meaningful to their customers. As opposed to conventional market research and focus group studies, the "ethnographic approach more closely matches the way people truly think and live."[5]

Ethnography is becoming increasingly important in the field of consumer insight, as more and more corporations are using ethnographers' valuable information to design more efficient, user-friendly, and localized adaptations of their products and services. This helps to avert marketing disasters and boosts risk management strategies.

Intel, for example, is now employing anthropologists and ethnologists in Asia in order to better understand the culture and behaviors of people in the various countries. In the West, where Intel is headquartered, individualism prevails, and Intel's products reflect this. However, in Asia, people are not first and foremost individuals; they are part of a family, a clan, a lineage, and they tend to share things a lot more. Intel is trying to understand this behavior in order to develop and market more products and devices that have multiple usage benefits. This is a part of the move toward mass customization that is replacing mass marketing.

Mass Customization

Mass customization is becoming more and more prevalent in the "Relationship Age." It is part of the democratization process of business, which is opening up channels for customers to express what they really want in terms of products and services. What used to be a privilege of the rich is being made available to all consumers—especially the young, who see it as a means to differentiate and express themselves. By this novel means, companies are attracting and empowering the unpredictable yet profitable Millennial market by personalizing the in-products of their generation, such as sneakers and digital iPods. According to Nike spokesman Alan Marks, the company has operated NIKEiD on nike.com since 1999 but relaunched it in March 2005 with more styles and new technology, enabling consumers to self-style products such as sneakers, bags, and golf balls.

Another major trend in world marketing is that of corporate social responsibility.

CORPORATE SOCIAL RESPONSIBILITY

Corporate social responsibility (CSR) is all about aligning corporate interests with consumer and employee welfare, by delivering value to the society at large as well as to shareholders.

The World Business Council for Sustainable Development (WBCSD) defines CSR as "the continuing commitment by business to behave ethically and contribute to economic development while improving the quality of life of the workforce and their families as well as of the local community and society at large."[6]

Research has shown that, in many organizations, there is a direct correlation between community-building initiatives, including the creation of relationships with customers through customized service, and a positive influence on profits. This phenomenon is hardly surprising given the current era of consumer concern and the communication revolution. In other words, companies that are sincere and genuine in their activities and with respect to consumer interests find that this pays dividends.

For example, The Body Shop, whose retail outlets and products are advocates for ecologically and ethically friendly cosmetics, spends little on advertising. The Body Shop is "a conveyor of a political philosophy of women, the environment and ethical business,"[7] and this corporate religion produces behaviors that reflect these concerns, which are intrinsic to the company's business activities.

Constant monitoring of opinion polls is crucial when taking a proactive stance on consumer issues. Such polls provide intelligent consumer insights and concerns, as opposed to the more superficial market research. Companies carrying out research on these issues will gain access to the valuable data required for public relations or community-building initiatives, which may result in meaningful long-term associations with customers when they act as advocates for consumer interests. Many companies today donate a certain percentage of their profits to charitable associations or causes such as funding HIV/AIDS awareness, health issues, fair labor practices, poverty eradication, community building, anti-discrimination, and environmental conservation measures. These cause-related marketing initiatives give companies the humanistic aura of a caring organization that can be more valuable than dollars spent on advertising.

CSR requires consistent and proactive associations with consumer issues, which will generate a powerful buzz among customers and create interest in the company's products or services. The immediate tangible value may be slow in coming, but the intangible values added to the brand will be enduring. The "United Colors of Benetton" campaigns of recent years made clear that the clothing company shared the same strong opinions on world issues as the Millennials. As a result of the positive publicity it received, the company became a marketing success story. (Eventually, it would overstep the bounds of respectability.) This trend for companies to link their brands and their marketing to beliefs and values that they hold in great esteem is known as cause-related branding or marketing.

Cause-related Marketing

The research paper "Brand Benefits" is the most holistic study ever carried out on the impact of cause-related marketing on consumers. Published by Business in the Community in October 2004 in association with Research International, Lightspeed Research, and relationship marketing specialist company Dunnhumby, the research covers the relationship between cause-related marketing, brand affinity, and brand equity, as well as the impact of cause-related marketing on actual consumer perception, loyalty, buying behavior, and the bottom line.

The research findings reveal the following:

- 98% of consumers in the United Kingdom and the United States are now aware of at least one cause-related marketing program, as compared with 88% in 2000.

- Over two-thirds of consumers (68%) are still calling for more companies to be involved in cause-related marketing.

- Seven in 10 consumers who had participated in a cause-related marketing program reported a positive impact on their behavior or perceptions.

- 48% of consumers reported an actual change in their behavior: they either switched brands, increased their usage, or tried or enquired about new products.

These findings illustrate the positive impact of CSR on consumers, as most people would be drawn to brands that are aligned with causes that are close to their hearts. The former UN secretary general, Kofi Annan, launched the Global Compact in 1999, urging corporate leaders to adopt its original nine principles espousing human rights, labor rights, and environmental responsibility. In their quest to achieve corporate goals, these organizations have to fulfill their corporate social responsibilities by providing solutions to social problems as well as strengthening the local economy. This global partnership program has garnered support from more than 300 corporations worldwide.

Benefits that corporations can expect to reap from CSR include the following:

- enhanced brand image and reputation
- improved customer goodwill and loyalty
- increased attractiveness to investors
- strengthened relationships with all stakeholders
- improved prospects for long-term financial and organizational success
- enhanced perception among communities and the public
- strengthened employee loyalty, commitment, morale, retention, and performance
- enhanced ability to attract more talented and motivated employees.[8]

Another major force influencing world marketing and the building of closer relationships is the advent of the Internet, digitalization, and interactive communication. These developments have helped marketers to get closer to youth than ever before, by demonstrating that they understand this new medium.

THE INTERNET AND DIGITALIZATION

As the world moves rapidly into the digital era, companies have to adapt to new ways of doing business, such as marketing on the Internet and other electronic media. Sophisticated information communication technologies drive these new marketing channels, and while many companies are happily adjusting to the changes, others are choosing to ignore them. With these new marketing channels, companies face the problem of re-creating the same relationships and associations with the consumer that they enjoyed while using the old marketing channels. For instance, the new channels don't facilitate face-to-face meetings of customers with company personnel, but instead allow customers to view products on a computer screen and to place an order online.

The potential of the World Wide Web shouldn't be underestimated. Many companies have already found innovative ways to exploit its potential. Marketers carefully monitor chat rooms and personal websites to gather information about their target market. Some even set up personal websites in order to pass on information about their brands. These sites pose as ones that are set up by a young person. When others enter these sites to chat, subtle information about the brand is passed on to the visitor during the course of the conversation.

Not all Web-marketing initiatives are non-intrusive in nature; some are quite open in the way they advertise themselves through search engines, Web banners, or pop-ups placed in other websites. However, the direct nature of this advertising gives the viewer a choice as to whether to view the material. Regardless of the method, the World Wide Web is a novel way to create a buzz about a new product, even before the actual product launch.

The Digital Revolution

The convergence of technology, the communications revolution, current events, and value drivers have determined that the "us" and "them" mentality of the "Transaction Age" has been replaced by the "togetherness" mentality of the "Relationship Age." Out of necessity in this current age, the top-down hierarchy system in companies has been largely replaced by the flattened organization. The "Relationship Age" promotes what Anthony Giddens calls "a society which is inclusive," a sort of "civic culture of global participation."

The fact is that consumers influence the business direction, and yet the decision-making power lies with organizations. The subtleties here lie in the fact that the communication revolution has laid bare all that can be bared, thereby empowering consumers and enabling them to take matters into their own hands. The worldwide free flow and sharing of information over the internet has broken down the formerly well-entrenched privacy barriers. The Millennials are truly a global generation, as the Internet enables them to connect and communicate with people from all over the world at breathtaking speed.

The scandals involving Martha Stewart, Enron, and WorldCom

in the United States have heightened distrust of corporations and highlighted consumers' need for transparency and accountability.

The growing distrust of the culture of corporate branding is well illustrated by the international anti-Nike movement. Nike's sweatshop scandals dating from the 1990s have been the subject of over 1,500 news articles and opinion columns. The company's Asian factories have been probed by cameras from nearly every major media organization. As a result, several people in Nike's PR department now work full-time dealing with the sweatshop controversy—fielding complaints, meeting with local groups, and developing Nike's response—and the company has created a new executive position: vice president for corporate responsibility.[9]

PR initiatives and the need to appear socially responsible are the prime movers of the "Relationship Age" from globalization toward de-globalization. Organizations now realize that their very continuation is established upon the trust of all quarters. The flow of information from within the organization to the outside world makes it susceptible to any bad press in relation to either consumers or employees. Companies are now more careful and proactive in their brand communications with respect to CSR, and use channels of communication to suit the preferences of their audiences.

Below are a few of the ways in which digital marketing techniques are influencing corporate marketing to youth.

Viral Marketing

Viral marketing is a non-intrusive, word-of-mouth marketing concept used by many marketers today. As is suggested by the name, word of the product is spread around in much the same way that the grapevine operates, using tools such as the Internet, mobile phones, and product placements in TV shows, movies, and games, as well as peer group catalysts. At its very simplest, it is "word of mouth" distributed via technology, but it is very powerful in its impact.

Viral marketing consists of messages that are passed on within the target market by peer group members, or those seeming to be part of the group. Essentially, it is using the consumer to spread the word. This marketing phenomenon came about in order to attract Millennials, who are extremely brand-conscious and yet have an aversion to direct advertising. Media proliferation and advertising have created a highly fragmented audience; hence the shift to consumer-to-consumer marketing, which is a cost-effective way to create a buzz and build brand awareness. Without proper planning, however, viral marketing can go awry, because the uncontrollable nature of "viruses" in itself reflects the essence of the empowered consumer.

Mobile Advertising

Most Millennials, even those as young as seven years, cannot do without their mobile phones. In the world of the Millennials, for whom text messages are the most common means of communicating with their peers, one could be a social outcast without a mobile phone. This dependence has become a boon for marketers, who are using this method to spread information about products and promotions via text messages that are being passed on by peers. Text messages also allow young people to interact and express their opinions about products and services with one another. Mobile advertising is a direct, personalized, interactive, and targeted form of communication between marketers and the consumer.

This close relationship could work to the disadvantage of marketers, as any bad press would spread rapidly, and thus requires careful planning and quality control. Although mobile advertisements are an effective marketing tool, a large number of ads may be considered intrusive unless one has obtained permission from the users themselves. Thus, "tie-ins" with phone companies are essential to avoid being accused of sending unsolicited messages (although there is some animosity toward operators who intrude themselves).

Mobilizing Catalysts

Mobilizing catalysts is a vital part of viral marketing; it involves appointing leaders of a community to generate a buzz within the group. Identifying leaders who have a respected voice, influencers, or trend-setters within the community, is crucial to this strategy. These leaders should be passionate about sharing their experiences or being brand ambassadors. They are usually proactive about building and nurturing relationships in the community around them and about issues that are close to their hearts. These relationships are usually based on trust, commitment, and mutual understanding; however, the strongest voice remains that of the catalysts. Thus, it is the catalysts, and not the brand, that take on the role of projecting a certain desired lifestyle to their peers.

Many marketers are hiring catalysts to spread the word about, or to promote, their brands among their peers. Celebrity endorsements apply this concept. A well-known illustration of this was the black urban rap group Run DMC prominently displaying their Adidas sneakers at their concerts. Tommy Hilfiger's clothing line also attracted similar acclaim, thanks to the rappers' penchant for the brand's outfits.

Mobilizing catalysts is all about mobilizing real people with whom others within the community can relate.

Alliances and Advergaming

The old saying that there is strength in numbers holds true in the present age of mutualism, when brands can no longer stand alone. This banding together of brands is inevitable, given the current glut of advertising and media messages. The very survival of some smaller brands lies in their collaborating with bigger ones or with brands within similar industries. Alongside the more traditional methods of product placements, event sponsorships, contests, and other co-branding efforts, of growing interest to marketers and youth is the relatively new practice of advergaming.

Advergaming is currently being touted as the future of

interactive advertising. The concept works much the same as product placement in movies and television programs, and involves placing brands strategically within the scenes of interactive games. Some brands are using this method as a viral marketing precursor to launch upcoming events.

In conjunction with the launch of Columbia Pictures' medieval action adventure movie *A Knight's Tale*, for instance, parent company Sony Pictures Entertainment launched an online competition called the "XJL"–the Extreme Jousting League. Gamers duelled in a "medieval, 3D jousting arena–with *A Knight's Tale* banners and ads posted liberally around the battlefield."[10]

Much like the "Matchbox" cars of old, which were miniature models of famous automobile brands, the electronic versions of brands create impressions and brand recognition in the minds of gamers spending time in virtual worlds. The setting of the game may include branded petrol and retail outlets, billboards, or even clothing and shoes worn by the characters involved. Microsoft's Xbox, Sony PlayStation, and Nintendo GameCube are all in contention for this lucrative market.

The advergaming concept was considered stimulation enough for Nike to create an advertisement with NBA basketball player LeBron James clad in Nike athletic wear battling it out in a mystical basketball game with a golden dragon. The advertisement created enough buzz to upset Chinese viewers, who considered the dragon to be sacred in their culture.

The point to note about the communications revolution in all its forms is that youth brands continually push the limits– sometimes they win and sometimes they lose. MTV always seems to push the limits, and indeed has its critics, but overall it manages to give its audience what they desire, which is why it has reached global status.

CONCLUSION: IT'S ABOUT EVOLUTION, NOT REVOLUTION

Given that change is occurring with lightning speed, brands have to be more nimble, more alert, more versatile, and more understanding, and be capable of evolving in line with the changes that are taking

place in the lives of young people today. Above all, it is essential to build emotional capital, as this translates to long-term brand building and customer loyalty.

But in adapting to constant change, world-class brand builders have recognized that brand management isn't about big swerves in brand behavior; it's about evolving the brand to keep abreast of customers' evolving lifestyles. Brands have to maintain relevance and build relationships if they are to win the hearts and minds of customers in the 21st century.

The rewards for good "Relationship Age" branding are many, but the main outcome is a global brand that has sustainable differentiation and loyalty.

From a commodity to a brand: that is MTV's achievement. Once you have been recognized by MTV, you have arrived. The sky is the limit; your dreams have come true, because the amount of airplay you receive on MTV will make you an instant global celebrity. Yes, you can rest easy once you have been recognized by MTV.

MTV has truly transformed the world's perceptions of music and pop culture. Combining music and television with an attitude and originality since 1981, MTV has been the voice of youth culture ever since.

But, as with all truly great brands, MTV has ensured that it has evolved its brand in line with people's changing lifestyles, needs, wants, and desires. Great brands aren't schizophrenic; rather, they grow with the consumer and reflect the ongoing changes in their lives. The following quotations illustrate that the brand has been constructed with meticulous precision and hasn't just stumbled on a few wild notions that it has executed well. MTV truly deserves its global success.

"Ours is a business of creative vision, smart brand building, unrelenting consumer focus and good execution," said Tom Freston, former MTV parent Viacom co-president and co-chief operating officer, in 2004. Judy McGrath, chairman and CEO of MTV, said of the company in 2004: "With more than 75 percent of MTV's channels outside of the United States, we are a truly global operation that is fueled by the exchange of creative ideas and cultures... I think our mantra has always been 'Evolve or die.'"

All aspiring global brands take note.

Consumer insight is critical to global brand building. In the next chapter you will read more about youth, and about how MTV has really understood what youth all over the world need and want.

[1] C. K. Prahalad and Venkatram Ramaswamy, "Co-Creation," http://www.12manage.com/methods_prahalad_co-creation.html.

[2] Martin Lindstrom and Patricia B. Seybold, *Brandchild: Remarkable Insights into the Minds of Today's Global Kids and Their Relationships with Brands*, (London: Kogan Page, 2003).

[3] Robert Polet, interview by Sarah Raper Larenaudie, *Time*, September 14, 2004.

[4] Paul Temporal, *Branding in Asia: The Creation, Development, and Management of Asian Brands for the Global Market*, Rev.Ed., (Singapore: John Wiley & Sons (Asia), 2001).

[5] *Margaret's Walking Stick*, Spring 2005, http://www.margaretswalkingstick.com/index.cfm?archive=4/1/2005.

[6] "Corporate Social Responsibility–Introduction," *tutor2u*, http://www.tutor2u.net/business/strategy/corporate-social-responsibility-introduction.html.

[7] Naomi Klein, *No Logo: Taking Aim at the Brand Bullies* (New York: Picador, 2000), p. 24.

[8] Philippine Business for Social Progress/United Nations Volunteers/New Academy of Business, "Enhancing Business–Community Relations: The Role of Volunteers in Promoting Global Corporate Citizenship," The Philippine Report 2003.

[9] Naomi Klein, *No Logo: Taking Aim at the Brand Bullies* (New York: Picador, 2000), p. 366.

[10] Christopher Saunders, "Offline Brands Turning to Advergaming," *ClickZNews*, 2001, http://www.clickz.com/showPage.html?page=725181.

MTV Shows
Music Videos Be on MTV
Live Performances
Genres
Shop MTV Shows
Europe Music Awards   MTV Shows Gossip
Shop

m t v

4

MTV and Global Urban Youth Culture

THE MILLENNIAL GENERATION: A PROFILE OF YOUTH TODAY

The Millennials—that is, those aged 15 to 34—are the generation of the "Relationship Age." They are considered to be more eclectic, diverse, and free, and more technologically perceptive, and hence better informed, than previous generations. It is generally estimated that at least 35% of Millennials worldwide are connected to the Internet, giving them instant access to huge amounts of information.

The Millennials are impassioned environmentalists, consider volunteerism to be "cool," distrust corporate globalization forces, and are averse to overt advertising. Ironically, they are also voracious consumers, having been exposed to brands from an early age. Thirty-nine percent of Millennials worldwide are from affluent households; thus, when compared to the general population, they have higher purchase intention and involvement across several categories. In Asia, for example, a 2003 survey of MTV's viewers in the 15–34 demographic indicated that Millennials are more likely to:

- own a PDA (Personal Digital Assistant)—31%
- own a PC/desktop computer—22%
- own a video camera—99%
- own a mobile phone—33%
- use perfume—41%
- use skincare products—36%
- use deodorant—36%
- drink fruit juice—26%
- drink carbonated soft drinks—17%
- play basketball—23%
- go to the cinema—100%
- have visited a cafe over the past months—56%
- have visited a fast-food restaurant over the past month—41%
- have visited a Western restaurant over the past month—20%
- have a car in the household—74%
- have traveled by air in the past year—46%.[1]

Recent research has shown that mobile facilities are going to play a greater role, not only in how youths communicate but also, in how they enjoy musical content. This will have an impact on traditional media such as television and MTV is recognizing this by building a digital strategy. This is discussed in more detail in Chapter 11.

Studies done for Nickelodeon found that kids aged 8-14 send an average 14.4 text messages and make 8.8 calls on their mobile phones every day. Jason Hirschhorn, MTV's chief digital officer, said, "Kids want their phones or their MP3 players to say something about who they are." MTV used this knowledge to help Virgin Mobile Holdings and handset maker Kyocera Corp. design a new slider phone.[2]

The Millennials don't form a homogeneous group and can be divided into general categories of young people, such as

- *Tween Girls (8–14):* Although still at the dawn of the trends curve, this group is a rising force in the marketplace. Most are brand-savvy and have a tremendous influence on personal as well as family purchases. Music, fashion, and other lifestyle-related brands are pertinent to this group. They represent every marketer's dream, as they spend nearly five times more than their male equivalents.

- *Tween Boys (8–14):* Boys will be boys, and these male counterparts of tween girls differentiate themselves from the girls by their interest in technology and sports. As tech-savvy as they are, they are more likely than girls to own computers, video games, and other gizmos. Sport features heavily with this group, who consider sports-related purchases such as football merchandise to be necessary.

- *Teen Girls (14–17):* The mid-teens are always considered the core of a trend. Being self-assured, smart, and early adopters, teen girls are usually trend-setters. As such, they mostly hover in groups, and the popular and "cool" ones become catalysts for trends, with their followers quickly adopting styles to avoid being social outcasts.

- *Teen Boys (14–17):* These tech- and media-savvy veterans form the core of a trend. Many possess personal spending money, which they spend on video games, sporting merchandise, and music. They are apt to spend their time watching TV, surfing the Net, and playing a physical sport as well as video games. Their brand-consciousness has been fine-tuned by their exposure to numerous brands from a young age, thus making them most likely to brand hop depending on which brand has the requisite style or technologically advanced edge.

Peer Pressure and Pragmatism

A particular feature of this generation is peer pressure, which helps form core trends. This dominant pattern diminishes in strength as a person gets older. This is especially so upon the onset of college and adulthood, when life's larger issues take precedence and trends become of secondary interest. The attitudes and approaches of the Millennials are mostly multicultural in nature, and they are comfortable in embracing diversity, perhaps reflecting the fact that at least 35% of the Millennials worldwide have an upper-secondary education and are connected to the world through the Internet.

Millennials are more apt to respond to humor and the unadulterated truth. Family ties and religious/spiritual values are on the rise among this generation in the aftermath of September 11 and the terrorist bombings in Asia and Europe. This trend is being reflected in the greater trust Millennials are placing in authority figures such as parents, teachers, and the police.[3] Songs about parental love and sacrifice—such as "You Raised Me Up" by Josh Groban and "I Turn To You" by Christina Aguilera—are typical of those that have made it on to MTV's play list in recent years.

Volunteerism is evident among Millennials, many of whom are spending time serving in their communities, or are contributing in cash or kind, or are even signing up for large-scale disaster relief efforts such as that following the 2004 Asian Tsunami. Undoubtedly, the Millennials are highly representative of the "Relationship Age" generation.

The Millennials are also conspicuously pragmatic when it comes to financial matters, having been given financial responsibilities and a say in family purchases such as cars, electronics, and groceries from a young age. This gives them much influential sway when it comes to the spending patterns of their parents and peers, and makes them strong brand advocates as long as the brands meet their needs. Many have long-term career and life goals with a view toward home ownership and other family commitments such as insurances.

Marketers who are receptive to these trends have capitalized on these shifts in demographics and psychographics. For example, in

Malaysia, property developers are building studio and one-bedroom apartments targeted at "a young population with 40% of the total population below 30 years of age and 20% below 20. As the young reach employment age, household formation will escalate."[4]

The tenets of the "Relationship Age" were built around the Millennials, who have raised the bar in lifestyle standards that envelop the realms of culture, literature, education, technology, entertainment, politics, business, fashion, and the arts. An overview of their main characteristics, from a branding and marketing perspective, follows.

THE UNIVERSAL CHARACTERISTICS OF YOUTH

Youth share several universal characteristics that lead to consistent behavioral patterns. It is important for a youth brand to understand these characteristics and patterns, as they present brand builders and marketers with some significant challenges. MTV has demonstrated an uncanny understanding of the universal characteristics of youth, which is one of the main reasons, I believe, it has become a global youth icon.

The Unreachable Generation: Complex and Difficult to Penetrate

The Millennial Generation is dynamic and organic in psyche, because they mature quickly and their changing tastes reflect their physical and psychological changes. Although they represent a huge prospective market, they remain extremely complex and difficult to reach using traditional marketing strategies.

The necessity for self-expression stems from this generation's desire for affirmation. The trend toward "experience" and "customization" in marketing has its roots in the attempts to fulfill the needs of the Millennials, who crave a personalized lifestyle. The experiential nature of the "Relationship Age" is pertinent to the active lifestyles of the Millennial Generation. They have high energy levels and love to indulge in endurance testing activities such as extreme sports. Their propensity to analyze information enables them to distinguish fact from fiction. This makes them early adopters, yet they are hard to please if things don't live up to their criteria. Once again, peer pressure factors largely in this equation.

Simon Williams, president and CEO of consultancy firm Sterling Brands, believes that what Millennials see as "cool" is in a state of flux, and that the concept is much more subtle than in the past. "Traditionally," Williams says, "being cool simply meant who you knew and what you wore; today, it's a much more multifaceted thing involving knowledge, attitude, behavior and visual cues— 'experiential cool,' in the marketers' jargon."[5]

Essentially, marketers who miss these cues, and thereby generate the wrong impression or communicate the wrong message, could lose this worldly-wise generation, resulting in the death of their brand. The values of youth—or, rather, of the Millennial Generation—center around the emotional realms of passion, honesty, and enduring relationships. They decry corporate irresponsibility, want complete transparency, and place a high value on close relationships that generate mutual respect and support.

Educated, and Tech- and Media-savvy

Social and intellectual capital have become the value drivers of the "Relationship Age." Knowledge that capitalizes on the wealth of practical experience has a powerful advantage over cold facts, and this has stimulated the argument for "continuous improvement" driven by creating meaningful experiences on both sides of the relationship. As Gary Marx says, "Unleashing and connecting the collective knowledge, ideas, and experiences of people creates and heightens value."[6]

Youth today have better access to higher education levels than preceding generations. Although up-to-date statistics are not yet available, by 2003 MTV knew that 67% of MTV viewers worldwide had an upper-secondary education. Educational trends are experiencing the shift from uniform education (a "one-type-suits-all" approach) toward personalized education, such as mastery educational systems or learning at your own pace, coupled with access to all the information available on the Internet; this has helped many young people reach and exceed intellectual standards not previously thought possible.

Youth today are much more informed at an earlier age as a result of their exposure to various types of media. Having grown up in a world of information overload, young people are very efficient in filtering out everything except information that is relevant to them. Millennials depend on multimedia technology such as television, Internet access, and mobile phones to support their lifestyles; for instance, they buy their movie tickets online or get the latest news updates through text messages. According to Martin Lindstrom and his co-writers/researchers, "Nearly half the world's urban tween generation have access to the Internet, and about 20% have their own mobile phone."[7]

Millennials are accomplished game wizards, Web designers, emailers, chat room participants, and bloggers. The demographics of Internet users among the Millennials worldwide range from the tech-savvy teen boys, and tween girls with mobile phones sending picture messages, in the West, to relatively conservative youngsters in Asia and Africa. Their ability to filter information has made Millennials familiar with the purpose and intent of communications. Hence, they are acutely aware of society's problems and injustices, and are insistent that solutions be found to social problems such as HIV/AIDS, war, discrimination, and poverty.

The Millennials have transformed the mass media into the media of the masses, which enables information to be disseminated at lightning speed all around the world. Many companies today, and especially the multinationals, track bloggings on the Internet to try and learn what people around the world are saying about them. By means of this global conversation and viral marketing techniques, corporations are not only finding out what the world is thinking, but have also found a way to help build brands and promote products. They have also learnt that young people today are extremely fickle.

Fickle-minded

The adage "here today, gone tomorrow" might have been coined to describe the fickle-minded Millennials, whose attention spans are very short where brands are concerned. Although they are avid consumers who are extremely brand- and image-conscious, much of the "flavor of the month" relates to their evolving tastes in media, music, sports, peers, and so on. Brands translate to a sense of identity that is extremely important to young people because it correlates to their sense of belonging—a type of herd mentality where peer pressure features prominently in their lifestyles.

Young people are exposed to thousands of brands every day. As they have significant spending power, and/or have the power to influence the spending of their families and friends, brands are a major part of their lives. The impact which youth, as trend-setters, have on consumer behavior overall—especially the purchase of clothing, music, accessories, and so on—has caused marketers to make these consumers a crucial part of their marketing initiatives.

With their growing numbers, and economic and cultural influence, Millennials have spawned the cradle-to-grave efforts of marketers. However, this is a double-edged sword, as marketers need to infuse brands into young people's lifestyles without being intrusive. Millennials don't like to be told to do something, or to be talked down to; as such, they are averse to direct advertising. Proactivity, combined with sensitivity to change and the propensity to innovate, is the winning formula for capturing the Millennials market.

Minding the generational gap also factors heavily in countering the fickleness of youth. Having been a dominant brand for too long can have its drawbacks, especially if it is associated with an older generation. Brands that are favorites of their parents may not appeal to young people. Levi's has experienced erosion in its market share in recent years due to the brand's association with the Millennials' parents, the baby-boomers and Generation X-ers.

As mentioned in Chapter 3, television and viral marketing efforts have created relationships with teens, as they see their favorite celebrities from the movies, music, and sport endorsing all sorts of brands, from clothing to games and drinks, in an acceptable way. Novel branding strategies such as advergaming (see Chapter 3) have taken unobtrusive youth marketing to new heights using product placements within game settings. Content providers for teen websites and chat rooms also have their hidden "agendas" when disseminating information.

Content features heavily in holding the attention spans of fickle youth, and content is a vital element in MTV's key point of difference. MTV's image, attitude, and originality, as reflected in its content, sets it apart in the highly saturated media market. "The network will continue to change with the times. I think our mantra has always been 'Evolve or die,'" said Judy McGrath, MTV Networks' chairman and CEO in 2004, In particular, MTV's ability to spot the difference between trends and fads has enabled the brand to keep up with rapid change and remain relevant to its market.

Trends and Fads: The Speed of Market Change

In response to the knowledge that youth is extremely tech- and fashion-savvy while having relatively short attention spans (the norm is to acknowledge that a product exists, adopt it for a while, and then move on to something new), brands have flooded the marketplace with new products with short product life cycles—just six to eight weeks, in some cases. The average product life cycle for technology is three to four months, while most fashion trends last from one to three months. Brand managers may therefore find it difficult to maintain their brands' relevance while enjoying continuity at the same time. The trick is to somehow lock into a fad and turn it into a trend.

A fad is something that has strong appeal to a very wide audience but which is short-lived; it may have a life span of a few months, say, and is usually associated with computer games, music, or fashion. Trends, on the other hand, start off as fads that appeal strongly to a very wide audience, but they then transcend time, either by maintaining their relevance or by returning time after time. Examples are flared jeans and tattoos.

For fads to develop into trends, they not only need to last longer—that is, to hold and stretch short attention spans—but also must create an emotional connection by becoming a staple with the user, which then translates into brand loyalty that stands the test of time. This also includes having the wide appeal of peer acceptance, as well as maintaining relevance in users' lives. For example, when the dot.com bubble burst, many companies got burnt, but out of those ashes emerged gems such as eBay and Amazon, who succeeded in making a connection with consumers through their novel ideas. The convenient and innovative choices, ideas, and services they offered to consumers generated a wide following worldwide.

Youth love fads because they are the ones that create them; as such, it's all about them. However, a fad will usually take off and gain acceptance only if it originates from the catalysts or the popular figures among the group. The MTV-introduced Aeropostale jeans made great headway into the American teen market because the commercials featured teens clad in the jeans while going about their daily routines. Much like a reality show, the only hint given that the footage was a commercial for the product was a fade-in of the brand name at the end of the commercial. The success of this campaign has propelled Aeropostale to an elite status among teen apparel brands.

Marketing to youth has always been more of an art than a science because of the difficulty in gauging whether a fad will eventually become a trend—or, indeed, whether or not it can be made into one. Apple's iPod caught on to the fad of downloading music from the Internet, thanks to Napster, and turned it into a trend. One of the things that MTV does very well, because of its intimacy with youth, is determining what will be a fad and what will become a longer-lasting trend. Hip-hop music and reality TV shows are examples of fads that MTV predicted early on would become trends. The virtual pet website, Neopets, an acquisition of MTV (described in Chapter 6), is another example.

It is a fine line to tread—some fads have become success stories, while others have faded away—but MTV is a master at turning fads into trends.

One of the main factors in relating to youth and generating long-lasting appeal is the concept of being "cool." If brand marketers don't understand what is "cool," they won't understand what will be fads and what will become trends; nor will they have any concept of where youth is going in its thinking and behavior.

The "Cool" Factor: Youth's Anti-establishment "Indie" Personality

"Indie" stands for independent. The "Indie" personality thrives on daring to be different from the crowd. It is a non-conformist attitude, where doing anything considered boring, predictable, or expected is seen as highly "uncool." Unique, funky people who are not afraid to be themselves are considered by their peers to be "awesome" and "cool."

It is considered "uncool" to be overtly associated with the establishment. "Indies" value empowerment, particularly as they are inclined to make their own choices and resent being told what to do. For a brand to be deemed worthy by "Indies," it has to create a bond with them by reflecting their lifestyles and understanding their needs and values in line with the demands of the "Relationship Age." Thus, it is vital that young consumers feel empowered or in charge, especially when they "discover" brands themselves or through word of mouth.

Above all, honesty and a brand "face" that identifies with and understands their personalities are success factors when relating to Millennials. It is all about "the real deal," which explains the success of unvarnished and unpolished reality television shows such as MTV's *Real World*. "We didn't have enough money to pay writers or hire stars," says Tom Freston, former Viacom co-president and chairman of MTV Networks. "So we came up with the idea of putting a bunch of young people in a loft and filming them. The series was called *Real World*. We had basically invented reality TV—although at the beginning it was purely a financial consideration."

An ironic twist to the "Indie" personality is the influence of peers in the choice of brands. Many young people would like to lay claim to the "Indie" personality, but the "cool" factor usually rides on the tides of the early trends adopters or catalysts. The world of the Millennials revolves around them. Advertisers and marketers need to penetrate their world, on their terms, if they are to have any chance of getting their message across to them. For this reason, outright advertising aimed at this generation more often than not misses its mark. Connected with this concept, and an important driver of the "cool" factor, is urban youth culture.

Urban Youth Culture

Urban youth culture is a significant trend-setter in its own right. Clothing, music, and accessories that are introduced and popularized in urban settings such as city streets and clubs permeate through to the larger youth market. The "hip" or trend-setter status of urban youth positions them as catalysts for many youth trends and brands. Their attitudes and values reflect diversity and multiculturalism, which is a critical element in the "Relationship Age."

Urban youth culture is generally associated with hip-hop music and dance, which is enjoyed by youth throughout the world; however, youth culture transcends music and permeates every aspect of their lives. Today, hip-hop has evolved into a multi-billion-dollar industry that inspires everything from fashion, mass-media marketing, and advertising, to sports. African-American rap music, which evolved from DJs "rapping" in rhyming "street" language about the reality of life in the ghettos, struck a chord with young people, who responded to both the rhythmic music and the sentiments expressed. The popularity of hip-hop today is reflected in the many white artists, such as Eminem, Justin Timberlake, and Britney Spears, who have ventured into what has traditionally been considered a black music domain.

Urban youth culture and street fashion were born out of the rappers' early inability to gain acceptance. However, that all changed in the mid-1980s when the group Run DMC was seen to promote Adidas sneakers at its concerts. Since then, fashion has come increasingly under the influence of urban youth culture, to the point where new ideas are played out almost from the moment they first appear on MTV. Hence, MTV is largely credited with the growth of "urban youth street vogue," through the hip-hop groups it

> Once Tommy was firmly established as a ghetto thing, the real selling could begin—not just to the comparatively small market of poor inner-city youth but to the much larger market of middle-class white and Asian kids who mimic black style in everything from lingo to sports to music.[8]

features on the channel. Today, black urban street wear sets fashion trends through the various nuances of black style, such as West Coast rap, hard-core, hip-hop, and rump shaking (popular in Miami). The Tommy Hilfiger brand became successful mostly due to hip-hop stars who had a fetish for its preppy look and baggy separates.

Ralph Lauren, Timberland, Reebok, and Nike have all ridden the urban street fashion wave because, as early adopters, the hip-hop artists are the first to embrace—or "blow up"—designer labels, bringing them into vogue with their fans and thus making them favored endorsers for many labels. The lure of urban street fashion is its ability to keep reinventing itself through appreciation of nuances and creativity.

Today, many celebrities have come up with their own fashion labels for footwear, jewelry, clothing, and even lingerie. Recording artists, Damon Dash, Jay-Z, and Biggs Burke created the Rocawear clothing line and Roc-A-Fella Records. Gwen Stefani has her L.A.M.B. collection of printed skirts, glamazon dresses, edgy sweaters, and rastastripe handbags; and Jennifer Lopez has Sweetface tops and dresses. Hip-hop mogul Russell Simmons set up Phat Farm, a leading urban clothing company worldwide. His wife Kimora Lee Simmons' Baby Phat, the first women's hip-hop label, designed the tiny T-shirts known as "baby tees." These hip-hop tzars, and others such as Sean John, formerly P. Diddy, (whose label is called "Sean John"), have created immense urban street fashion empires.

The "Relationship Age" is embodied in this urban youth market, with Millennials' love of diversity and self-expression, and their bold, in-your-face, sexy, and defiant attitudes, allowing them to see the world on their own terms. Beyoncé Knowles, former lead singer of the female R&B group Destiny's Child and now a global star in her own right, said of the 2005 "Destiny Fulfilled...And Lovin' It" tour, during which the group was dressed by the House of Deréon fashion label: "Performing is not only about sharing my musical passions, but it's also about expressing my individuality. By having Destiny's Child wearing House of Deréon on the tour, I am able to express my creativity and love of music and fashion."

The status of the urban youth market as an important catalyst of youth trends in fashion and music is undeniable. MTV's role as the groundbreaking standard-bearer of this important aspect of youth culture is reinforced through the promotion of its stars on the music channel. The far-reaching influence of MTV's global status has made it a major proponent of urban youth culture.

Metrosexuality

Another offshoot of the Millennial generation is the metrosexual male. The term *metrosexual* was coined by the media to describe modern masculinity as defined by young men who spend money on fashion and beauty products, as well as on entertainment and fitness, as a form of self-expression. The Millennials' breadth of knowledge has increased the fashion awareness of males in recent years. Metrosexuals are acutely aware of their appearance and think nothing of having facials, spa treatments, and massages, in order to make the most of their looks.

Metrosexuals aren't confined to the worlds of fashion, music, and the media; many are to be found in professions ranging from male-dominated sports to information technology. The movement also has a following among younger males, who take their lead from sports icons such as David Beckham, England's former football captain and now US soccer celebrity (a brand in his own right), whose changing hairstyles, diamond earrings, and fashionable clothing are testament to his metrosexuality. Long-established fashion house Abercrombie & Fitch even targets this particular market for its rugged, casual clothing lines by using terms such as *sex appeal, attitude, college, athletic logo,* and *celebrity* in its advertising.

The genre of music popular with this demographic is usually along the lines of contemporary pop, typified by boy band groups such 'N Sync, 98 Degrees, and Backstreet Boys, where the emphasis

> " The O-Town offensive has become one of the most elaborate star-making campaigns of the modern media age. The machinery seems to have paid off. In its first week of release, according to SoundScan, O-Town's self-titled debut CD sold 144,000 copies, entering at No. 5 on the charts.[9]

is on physicality rather than talent. The MTV-produced ABC show *Making the Band* followed the transformation of the five-piece boy band O-Town into a pin-up group.

Most of these boy bands have a short shelf life; they fall from grace as soon as the next fad, or flavor in "bubblegum" pop groups, comes around. But for a brief time, their metrosexuality– an attractive physique and appearance, charisma and glamor, combined with a fashion makeover and a hip song–makes them the darlings of teenage girls–and boys–and hence of brands targeting these markets.

In the next section of this chapter, we will examine some of the similarities and differences between global youth and Asian youth.

GLOBAL VERSUS ASIAN YOUTH CULTURE

Young people the world over have some values and behaviors in common, as described above, shaped to a large extent by the process of globalization. However, Asian youth still differ in many significant ways from their Western counterparts. MTV has managed to use these differences to its advantage.

> Global teens are a group with shared behaviors and purpose, yet remain loosely organic in their structure and potential evolution.[10]

Global Similarities
Globalization and the Communications Revolution

The Millennial Generation is generally identified as being more culturally ambiguous in nature than previous generations. Globalization and the communications revolution have brought about a greater mix of cultures. Global Millennials are characteristically neither race- nor gender-focused, but display a great interest in human issues such as social and environmental concerns. For example, Asian youth today are adopting

> Youth are more culturally absorbent than their parents. While adults may harbor traditional customs and ways, global teens shed those pesky national hang-ups like last year's fashions. Despite different cultures, middle-class youth all over the world seem to live their lives as if in a parallel universe. They get up in the morning, put on their Levi's and Nikes, grab their caps, backpacks and Sony personal CD players and head for school ... [where they are] more likely to wear the teen "uniform" of jeans, running shoes, and denim jackets... They are also more likely to own electronics and consume teen "items" such as candy, sodas, cookies, and fast food. They are also more likely to use a wide range of personal care products too.[11]

many Western mannerisms in their tastes for music, fashion, entertainment, and technology; while Western youth are becoming increasingly fascinated with ethnic Asian and African fashion and musical trends as they broaden their worldview. Hence, today's youth are more globally inclined, with technology, global brands, and the English language playing an important role in their lives.

Newspapers have recorded a drop in sales, as most Millennials prefer to read the latest news online. Watching movies and playing games online is second nature to them. Mobile phones are their preferred means of communication. Phones must be equipped with the "basics" of MMS (Multimedia Messaging Service), WAP (Wireless Application Protocol), or GPRS (General Packet Radio Service), which include games, mobile chatting, and text messaging, as well as downloads such as ringtones, logos, screensavers, and other accessories. They have even developed a global language among themselves that is suited to mobile technology and online chatting.

The Internet has enabled youth to extend their networks and connect with their peers outside of their immediate physical environment. This has given them a broader outlook and enriched their lives through their access to different people, different lifestyles, and new information. The Internet has enabled youth to reach out and duplicate the behaviors of their peers from across the globe. Virtual bodies, or "avatars," represent participants in the social environment of cyberspace or the World Wide Web. Although located physically in many parts of the world, youth can converge on a shared space daily despite differences in their language, culture, and time zone. This regular convergence has created a culture of shared behaviors and purposes, making cyberspace a world of its own and one devoid of boundaries.

This phenomenon has contributed to turning local trends into global ones, and vice versa, in short spaces of time. The recent trend of wearing rubber "idea" bracelets is a case in point, with young people collecting and wearing the bracelets to show their support for various causes. Global companies have incorporated this trend into their coporate social responsiblity (CSR) initiatives. Examples include Nike's "Stand Up Speak Up" Football Against Racism black-and-white intertwined wristbands, worn by footballers Thierry Henry and Ronaldinho in Europe, as well as the yellow Lance Armstrong "LiveStrong™" bracelet sold to raise money for cancer research. MTV's support for the "ONE Campaign," which aims to eradicate global poverty, is symbolized by its white wristband. Profits from the sale of these wristbands are contributed to the cause.

> Such messages are highly favoured by young people in an age when each of them is seeking an identity to set themselves apart from the pack... Nicholas Yap Tze Sheng, 18, is banded each day with a different colour... The wristbands appealed to him he said after he saw his favourite footballer Thierry Henry from English League club Arsenal wearing an intertwined black and white band during a match in support of an anti-racism campaign.[12]

Celebrities such as Britney Spears, Lindsay Lohan, US President Bush, and 2004 presidential candidate John Kerry, as well as numerous Olympic athletes, were seen sporting these "idea" bracelets in support of such causes. Given their ability, through the Internet and text messaging, to spread the word instantly about issues and brands, the Millennials are a force to be reckoned with.

Music and Media

The common thread that binds Millennials together throughout the world is music. Popular and urban music culture has produced "idols" young people strive to imitate; in this way, music is the basis for global youth culture, including young people's mannerisms, fashion statements, values and opinions, and the ways in which they interact with one another.

Most young people listen to music out of habit, for relaxation, or even to relieve boredom, but mostly to be part of a happening crowd. Most of them buy CDs frequently from music stores in malls or download music from the Web, and they tend to have similar tastes in popular music, particularly in the urban and rock genres. Some have even adopted the terminology and slang used by their musical "idols" as a lingua franca, enabling them to communicate with their peers worldwide. Many claim not to be able to live without music, which has opened the way for early adoption of new mobile products such as iPods, mobile phones, and PDAs, which make music available on demand.

TV tops the list of media avenues, as most urban Millennials worldwide have access to cable TV in their homes or even in their own rooms. Many of them keep up with the latest music—and, by extension, with what is currently "cool"—by this means; hence the popularity of MTV. It is the world's largest television network and the leading multimedia youth brand. In Asia, it is viewed by more young adults than any other music channel, reaching in excess of 180 million households across the region.

Young people's loyalty to MTV is a result of the network's ability to produce programming and content that appeal to them, by reflecting their music, including both international and local favorites, and their lifestyles. MTV's jam-packed 24/7 music programming makes it the preferred music channel for global youth, with shows such as:

- *Artist of the Month*
- *TRL*
- *Punk'd* (a successful program in which celebrities have pranks played on them)
- *BUZZworthy*
- *MTV Pop 10*
- *MTV Movie Awards*
- *This Is...* (a show featuring the history of contemporary bands such as White Stripes)
- *MTV Amplified* (formerly known as *MTV Rock It!*)

➤ *Hip Hop Countdown*
➤ *MTV Hits* (favorite hits and latest videos played back-to-back)

While some shows are shown across many countries, MTV also has specific programs for individual countries such as Malaysia, Indonesia, and the Philippines. *MTV Jus*, for example, features the latest Malay songs.[13]

In MTV's own words, "Music plays a key role in the lives of young people." Today's youth are progressive, sophisticated, and discerning; and they want to share their views and opinions about music and their musical "idols" with their peers worldwide. Thus, with its array of possible role models, opinion leaders, and spokespeople, music can play a key role in building brands, as it creates an emotional link, thereby building relevance in the lives of youth.

Cultural Differences between Asian and Western Youth

With around 1.3 billion people aged 15–34, representing approximately 36% of the total Asian population, Asia is the growth market of the future. Since most Asian youth consume a large proportion of their families' incomes, it is imperative that brands understand the mindset of this target market.

Even in the seemingly global uniformity of cyberspace, the Millennials remain ethnographically diverse. This stems from their sense of identity with their own culture, and influences marketers in the approach to globalization–localization of brand communications.

Individualist West versus the Collectivist East

The emphasis on "we" in the collectivist East is in contrast to the "I" mindset of the individualist West. The propagation of self over the group in individualism manifests in vocalization of individuals' opinions, maintaining private domains, decisions that benefit the individual and their immediate family, and the ultimate goal of

> Conformance to group behavior and group norms will be important in collectivistic cultures and the opinions of elders are more relevant than in individualistic cultures.[14]

self-actualization as envisioned by Maslow's hierarchy of needs theory. By contrast, the negation of individual identities in the collectivist East correlates to loyalty of the individual toward the vast societal and family system to which he or she belongs.

Despite collectivism and the traditional family values of the East, Asian youth are beginning to experience a shift in identity. This move toward modern pragmatism is the result of powerful global influencers—in particular, technology, music, and education. Many brands have begun to adapt these global influencers to local contexts, making them more meaningful to local consumers. For example, many global brands with local adaptations have been embraced by locals, because these brands were able to fit into their culture and lifestyle. Thus, customization to meet local tastes, spiritual beliefs, national character, education, rituals, and culture has become the norm.

Changing Psychographics of Asian Youth

As is the case with their counterparts in the West, technology and music feature heavily in the psychographics of Asian youth, many of whom possess mobile phones and have access to the Internet, thus giving them access to the latest media sources. In India, for example, youth have access to media sources ranging from newspapers and television to the Internet, giving them opportunities to interact with their peers and to gather information from all over the globe. As a result, they have a broad outlook and express their opinions on a range of issues that affect their lives, such as environmental concerns.

The Asian media is generally regarded as being controlled by government, unlike in the West where there is an inherent belief in the right to freedom of speech. The fact that most Asians seem resigned to this situation perhaps stems from the collectivist mindset of the East, where "eclecticism" and "pragmatism" for the greater good of society are valued more highly than "truth."

Many of these attitudes are eroding, especially among the "worldly-wise" Millennials who are being exposed to a virtual tsunami of media avenues. This proliferation of media is generally attributed to the changing psychographics of Asian youth, who are becoming notably more aggressive, independent, and competitive than were previous generations. For the first time in authoritarian China, Cantopop stars have replaced revered political leaders and elders as teen "idols."

Although they are still highly respectful of their elders, and although family ties remain relatively strong and rebellion has yet to take root, many Asian youths have become decidedly more materialistic in their outlook, favoring global brands and adopting Western mannerisms in their lifestyles, including going clubbing and attending parties. Sexual taboos seem to be eroding as well, as is evident in the increasing incidences of sexually transmitted diseases such as HIV/AIDS. While not yet quite out in the open, dating and premarital sex are quite prevalent in Asia, but most conservative societies in the region still frown on unmarried couples living together.

Brands, by association and purchase, give Asian youth a degree of social standing, in that they wear a brand as a badge of quality. For example, Japanese youth are the technology trend-setters of Asia. They set the standards with Pokémon (Pocket Monsters) figures and trading cards, videogames, and plastic superheroes. Their obsession with videogaming has spawned the rise of *The Legend of Zelda* and *Banjo-Kazooie* videogame series. These tech-savvy trend-setters are positively helping to prop up Japan's stagnant economy via the videogames of the entertainment industry.

Despite pockets of brand awareness such as those in Japan, the pervading collectivist mindset of Asian society determines that

Asian youth are averse to the risk of being trend-setters. Their need to conform to their peers makes them hesitant to try out new brands until, through media exposure or word of mouth, they are assured of the popularity of the brand. The inherent discouragement of individual identities in Asian society renders the concept of brand personalities an alien or Western phenomenon. Nonetheless, Asian youth are beginning to grasp the concept that brands have unique personalities; albeit, they are generally deemed functional, rather than experiential.

Local Still Rules

Cutting through all the hype about globalization, Asian youth remain localized at heart. It is this sense of identity and belonging that "anchors" them in their particular society. A case in point is India, where music spawned by Bollywood (the largest film industry in the world) is by far the leading genre among Indian youth. Even the mighty MTV was in danger of being upstaged by Bollywood's song-and-dance numbers. At the risk of being left behind, MTV decided to incorporate local elements into MTV India's content. Despite fears that this move might dilute the brand, it has propelled the station to greater heights.

Generally, Asian youth—especially those from India and China—remain fiercely loyal to the local elements of their culture, despite being clad in blue jeans and with a penchant for Coca-Cola and Western food. In Southeast Asia, especially in multiracial societies such as Singapore and Malaysia, foreign youth culture and music are taking precedence over the underdeveloped local music industry. Ironically, however, some local artists from this region, as a result of being featured on MTV, are now gaining greater regional exposure.

MTV has shown itself to be highly successful in understanding the complexity and diversity of youth culture, but how does it manage to stay on top when that culture changes so quickly?

> Standing triumphant at the center of [the] global teen phenomenon is MTV... the single most significant factor contributing to the shared tastes of the middle-class teens it surveyed was TV—in particular MTV, which 85% of them watched every day... A public address system to a generation. Global teens watch so much MTV per day that the only equivalent shared cultural experience among adults occurs during an outbreak of war when all eyes are focused on the same CNN images.[15]

RIDING THE WAVES AND STAYING ON TOP

Few brands stand the test of time and maintain their positions as influential forces in the lives of consumers. Strangely enough, MTV, as a 25-year-old, has managed still to be perceived as "cool" by viewers nearly half its age the world over. The secret of MTV's success is its innovative content, use of technology, programming and marketing strategies, and its ability to remain relevant to the lifestyles of its viewers wherever in the world they might be—from Timbuktu or Thailand or the United States. MTV's ability to relate to universal youth values has made it a compelling and unifying global youth icon.

CONCLUSION

There are four main drivers for the needs and wants of youth; they are:

- Entertain me.
- Inform me.
- Interact with me.
- Innovate for me.

MTV has a keen perception of the wants and needs of youth and it delivers on each of them.

When youth want to be entertained, they look to MTV for the best and latest music, visuals, and styles. MTV's take on modern lifestyles keeps its viewers informed about global trends and youth culture, which in turn helps shape their worldview and forges common traits among them. The interactivity of the MTV brand creates two-way connectivity, which is also a prerequisite of the "Relationship Age." Finally, MTV's constant momentum is the channel's way of keeping up with the demands of the Millennial Generation, who require an innovative medium to hold their attention.

In the next chapter we will examine how MTV has shaped its brand to reflect, attract, and keep its global and Asian youth customer base.

[1] Nielsen Media Index 2003 (Korea, Singapore, Indonesia, Philippines, Thailand); Cabsat 2002/03 (Malaysia, Hong Kong). (Note that the percentage of young MTV viewers in Asia owning a mobile phone would likely be far higher today.)

[2] Tom Lowry, "Can MTV Stay Cool?," *BusinessWeek,* February 20, 2006, http://www.businessweek.com/magazine/content/06_08/b3972001.htm.

[3] Applied Research & Consulting LLC.

[4] Interview with Datuk C. K. Wong, senior managing director, Sunway City Berhad: "Building Image to Win Market Share," StarBiz, *The Star,* July 20, 2005.

[5] "The Coolest Trends," *Business Line-Internet Edition,* http://www.hindu.com/businessline/2000/07/23/stories/102344g2.htm.

[6] Gary Marx, "Ten Trends: Educating Children for Tomorrow's World," *Journal of School Improvement,* 3, no. 1 (Spring) 2002.

[7] Martin Lindstrom and Patricia B. Seybold, *Brandchild: Remarkable Insights into the Minds of Today's Global Kids and Their Relationships with Brands,* (London: Kogan Page, 2003).

[8] Naomi Klein, *No Logo: No Space, No Choice, No Jobs,* "Alt.Everything - The Youth Market and the Marketing of Cool", (New York: Picardo 2002), p. 76

[9] Warren Cohen, "O-Town: Building the Perfect Boy Band," *Inside,* http://wjcohen.home.mindspring.com/insideclips/otown.htm.

[10] *Margaret's Walking Stick,* http://www.margaretswalkingstick.com/index.cfm?archive=3/1/2004.

[11] Naomi Klein, *No Logo: No Space, No Choice, No Jobs,* "Patriarchy Gets Funky – The Triumph of Identity Marketing", (New York: Picardo 2002), p. 119

[12] Chin Mui Yoon, *Star Metro,* Malaysia, September 15, 2005.

[13] More information on specific country-related shows can be found at www.
mtvasia.com/Onair/Shows/.

[14] Marieke de Mooij, *Global Marketing and Advertising: Understanding Cultural
Paradoxes* (Thousand Oaks, CA: Sage Publications, 1998).

[15] Naomi Klein, *No Logo: No Space, No Choice, No Jobs*, "Patriarchy Gets
Funky – The Triumph of Identity Marketing", (New York: Picardo 2002),
p. 120

MTV Shows
Music Videos Be on MTV
Live Performances Downloads Artist Photos Genres
Shop MTV Shows Show Photos
Europe Music Awards MTV Shows Gossip
Vid Charts
Shop

5

MTV Brand Anatomy

The heart of the MTV brand is summed up in the title of the song by Alphaville, "Forever Young." But before we take a closer look at this concept, we will consider how powerful brands like MTV are built.

A BRIEF INTRODUCTION TO BRAND BUILDING

Real global brands (brands that are accessible in most parts of the world) are few and far between. Those that have made it to global status tend to have been built conscientiously and carefully to match the values and desires of their intended customers. MTV is no exception to this rule. Nearly all of the big brands have three main characteristics in common.

First, there is some kind of vision or mission for the brand—a sense of purpose, and an articulation of what the brand wants to stand for emotionally in the minds of its customers. This is usually different from a corporate vision or mission. For example, the Hallmark brand stands for "enriching lives" and doesn't mention its business competencies; and Nike is all about winning and getting the best out of oneself, not about sportswear. This is sometimes called the "essence" of the brand—an emotional distillation of what it stands for.

Second, there is a set of brand values, often in the form of personality traits that guide the brand in its pursuit of its overall purpose. Again, corporations often have both corporate values and brand values. Corporate values are basically about how the company should behave internally, and here we find words such as "integrity," "respect," and "teamwork." Brand values are more outwardly directed and often assume words related to personality traits. Harley-Davidson, for instance, built a brand personality that matches its target audience by studying the attitudes, interests, opinions, and behaviors of the "big bikers" (namely, macho, male, enjoys heritage, loves freedom, patriotic). Levi Strauss does the same with its corporate and product brands. Most power brands have a personality all of their own.

The third characteristic global brands have in common is brand positioning, which really describes why the brand is different from and better than its competitors. For example, Nokia positions its brand as the only one possessing "human technology" that enables people to get the most out of their lives.

These elements form the basis of brand strategy, as opposed to business strategy, and they tend to be largely consistent over time. The vision and values/personalities of brands are long-term characteristics and don't change, just like people's vision and values/personalities don't change. Positioning can change, however, as markets are dynamic, and customer wants and needs, and competitor activities, can change.

Let's see how MTV has built its brand—what it stands for, its values, and its positioning.

THE MTV BRAND VISION: FOREVER YOUNG?

In his quest to be forever young, the Babylonian king Gilgamesh sought the waterweed that was believed to be a source of eternal youth, only to realize that the only immortality human beings can aspire to is to make names for themselves as builders of cities. Comedian and filmmaker Woody Allen takes the opposite view. "I don't want to achieve immortality through my work," he says. "I want to achieve it through not dying." Whoever one concurs with, the essence of eternal youth lies in the regeneration of the mind.

Neuroscientist Ian Robertson, dean of research at the Trinity College Institute of Neuroscience, in Dublin, Ireland, has offered a more pragmatic solution to the problem: "The brain is plastic shaped by what we do... The idea is to shake the brain out of lazy habits and return it to the way it was in youth... Continued learning and mental stimulation are also key to retaining ability, because they 'literally grow your brain.'"

In looking at the MTV brand, there doesn't appear to be any formally stated brand vision, but if we wish to interpret the brand in terms of what it stands for emotionally in the minds of consumers, I see a brand vision of being "Forever Young." These are my words, not MTV's, but this simple concept appears to drive everything that MTV does.

The MTV Brand Mission

MTV does have a formal brand mission, which is:

> To connect with our audience in a way that fuels their passions for music and challenges their thinking with the kind of fresh, relevant, risk-taking entertainment found nowhere else.[1]

MTV's elixir of eternal youth has proven to be reinvention and staying in touch with its audience through continuous learning and improvement. By keeping abreast not only of music, but also of trends and other issues pertaining to youth culture, MTV has transcended and elevated its status to a lifestyle brand. This achievement is realized through constant activity and interaction with its young audience, as Cristian Jofre, former senior vice president and creative director for MTV Networks International, explains:

> Everyone thinks we have a great job [at MTV] but we spend all of our time thinking, thinking. All the time trying to reinvent ourselves. We have to stay in touch with our audience without getting older. Always, we are studying trends, knowing what the kids are hearing and what the kids are watching on TV. We can talk with kids on a different level than other brands do, because in the end not everybody is targeting young people as specifically as us. We are in touch with the kids all of the time. Music is bigger than the musicians playing. At least for our audience, it is something bigger. It's about trends, it's about the way that you dress, it's about your friends, it's about the clubs; it's about all that.

MTV does more than merely care about what young people as a whole think; through its localized research and execution strategies, it seeks to understand the viewpoints of urban and rural youth, well-heeled and underprivileged youth, males and females, straights and gays, of every nationality and culture on the planet.

MTV'S CORPORATE AND BRAND VALUES/PERSONALITY

Until 2004, MTV had the following corporate values/personality attributes that it used to express its brand and interact with its youth audience:

- innovative
- interactive
- entertaining
- humorous
- music authority
- aspirational
- friendly
- stimulating
- WQ (weirdness quotient)
- colloquial.[2]

More recently it has changed its values to make them more relevant to the world of the consumer, but essentially the spirit of the brand remains the same. You will read more about these subtle changes in Chapter 11.

The MTV brand personality is the set of traits that we are more familiar with, as these are the traits MTV wishes to project to its target audience. They are delivered through its content, VJ strategies, special events, and lifestyle activities, and help to build the MTV character that differentiates it from competitors and conveys its position as a leader of youth culture. MTV's personality embodies the dynamic and high-energy nature of young people, being:

- relevant
- passionate
- unpredictable
- clever
- really funny
- risk-taking
- bold
- open
- no bullshit[3]

The "relevant" and "passionate" characteristics create the sense of personal connection with its viewers. The freshness of the MTV brand is communicated through its unpredictable, bold, clever, risk-taking, and really funny content. Like most young people when together, MTV is very open and doesn't tolerate bullshit. So, the MTV brand personality has been deliberately constructed to mirror that of its customers—youth. This helps define the unique character of MTV, just as your personality defines your unique character.

The essence of youth that embodies all these characteristics forms the heart of the MTV brand. The MTV difference is to remain youthful and relevant to its audience, no matter from which part of the world they originate.

The "cool," yet easy-going aura exuded by MTV appeals to youth all over the world, because it reflects what is both "cool" and relevant to them, wherever they may be. The key is to interpret what "cool" really means to each local audience, and this aspect of the MTV brand is addressed throughout this book.

Brand Image: The Personality Perceived Across Multiple Audiences

In terms of image (how the brand is actually seen), MTV's general persona is an ethnically diverse 24-year-old (the average age of an MTV viewer), who could be American born or from Hong Kong. But its personality is seen slightly differently in different Asian countries, as it presents itself to those audiences with relevance to their stage of development. (This topic is examined in more detail in later chapters.) So, in Southeast Asia, the key personality traits perceived are: relevant, risk-taking, bold, innovative, and open. MTV hopes to add "humorous" and "accessible" over time.

The changing face of MTV is powered by customized programming tailored specifically to serve its increasingly diverse, multi-ethnic, and cross-cultural global audiences. MTV's "think glocal" (think global, act local) strategy began when the channel realized in the late 1980s, during its process of global expansion, that "one size doesn't fit all."

MTV Asia alone has several localized channels that are in confluence with regional programming. This means that MTV's signature programs—such as *TRL*, *Trippin'* and *The Osbournes*—have to coexist with, or sometimes play a secondary role to, Bollywood numbers in India, Cantopop shows in China or Taiwan, or the Muslim call to prayer in MTV Indonesia, as described in an earlier chapter. Thus, content and editorial independence play a major role in shaping the brand personality of MTV's various outposts.

Frank Brown, former president of MTV Networks Asia, said at the C21 World Marketing Conference held in 2000: "It's very important that what we're going to market in each country fits with the local culture."

In substance, the MTV personality is clever and risk-taking, in that it sometimes breaks the rules in order to keep the brand fresh with programs such as *MTV Amplified*, *Pop Inc*, *Pimp My Ride*, *Punk'd*, and *Boiling Point*. Its sense of humor not only has to be entertaining and funny, but on the verge of the unexpected and even whacky. *MTV Bakra* on MTV India, hosted by VJ Cyrus Broacha, is a case in point. "*Bakra*" means "goat" in Hindi. Host Cyrus, who is immensely popular in India, plays pranks on celebrities. The humor and WQ (weirdness quotient) elements are pushed to the limits, reflecting the bold, risk-taking nature of youth.

Another characteristic of MTV is its interactivity. Programs such as *TRL*, *Pop Inc*, *MTV Hits*, and *VJ Hunt* aim to bridge cultural gaps and reach out to youth everywhere through the universal language of music. The interactive aspect of these programs gives the viewer a sense of aspiration, empowerment, and stimulation, as well as the assurance that MTV, the foremost authority on popular music, is listening to them.

MTV's vibrant, friendly persona and easy charisma, coupled with its ability to provide a 360-degree and 24/7 music experience, have earned it worldwide recognition.

The chapter will now examine how the MTV brand is positioned, and the benefits it provides for its viewers.

MTV'S GLOBAL POSITIONING

MTV has a great deal of depth in terms of how it links its mission and personality to its positioning in the marketplace. MTV is deeply committed to its involvement with millions of young people the world over, who need to see their hearts and souls reflected in a place that they can call their own. MTV makes young people feel the way they should feel: important, boundless, and real, as well as being close to their heroes and their dreams.

Not many companies can claim to be number one, but when they are first into the market, particularly with the introduction of a revolutionary new product, they are seldom forgotten. As the first mover in music television, MTV is widely regarded as the market leader. It continues to own this position because of the continuous learning approach it takes toward its programming mix, its content, and its external operations. This innovative attitude and outlook impacts on the brand. MTV innovates every minute of every day; not just every year, or every month.

Elements of MTV's Brand Positioning

MTV describes its positioning as being "totally devoted to young people through music, personal connections and a voice for youth culture." The three key elements are:

➤ It celebrates today's music experience.
➤ It provides a personal connection with young people.
➤ It expresses the attitudes, styles, and interests of today's generation of youth culture.

Let's take a look at what each of these elements of the positioning means.

Celebrating Today's Music Experience

MTV is referred to as "the home of music," because music is the foundation upon which the brand drivers are built. Since music is so close to the heart of youth, it presents an opportunity to own the youth mindset. Hence, MTV's celebration of the music experience is essentially a celebration of the global language of youth. The creative use of music re-energizes or creates new possibilities for the role of music.

The freshness of the brand is conveyed by using music that is cleverly crafted to package shows. Although no longer shown since 2005, *Rouge*, MTV Southeast Asia's first-ever regional drama series, was a good example of where music was used to set the tone for a show. The cast comprised five young women scouted from around the region and the United States. A team of highly experienced scriptwriters and talented musicians from Singapore created world-class content and upbeat, original music tracks that set the stage for the action and drama. The show centered on the women, who were compelled to work together despite their diverse cultural backgrounds and personal differences. The wardrobes and accessories were provided by the leading watch, accessory, and apparel label FOSSIL, the show's sponsor. Said Mark Parker, FOSSIL's senior vice president—Asia:

> We are proud to be associated with *Rouge* and are excited at the opportunity of being a part of this unique and creative project. *Rouge* provides a compelling platform to showcase FOSSIL's portfolio of watches, accessories, and apparel to the trendy young people of Asia. We are looking forward to leveraging this opportunity to fortify our position as the market leader in fashion accessories predicated on design and value.

This non-intrusive weaving of brands into programs reiterates that brand preferences often correlate with musical tastes; this is especially so for young people, for whom music plays a key role, not just in providing entertainment but in depicting their lifestyles.

MTV's role as the medium between celebrities and viewers is further augmented through its lifestyle programs, such as *The Ashlee Simpson Show, Cheyenne, Footballer's Cribs, MTV Cribs, The Osbournes*, and others which take audiences into stars' homes and private lives. MTV takes its celebration of the music experience a step further by giving viewers direct, intimate access to artists, as well as opportunities to live the life of a star—at least for a brief period—through its various contests. (See Chapter 8 for further examples.)

MTV's unique portfolio of musical events isn't confined to music videos; it is also showcased through original concerts and live performances, such as *Unplugged*—a live musical performance in an intimate setting, so that audiences are placed close to the artist, who performs without any accompanying electric instruments.

Musical "greats" such as Eric Clapton, Paul McCartney, Mariah Carey, and Grammy award-winning R&B diva Alicia Keys have all graced the *Unplugged* stage. Keys has commented that getting close to the audience enables her to project a "personal, soulful, and heartfelt feel" that "speaks to the audience," who can "understand what provoked her to write the songs."

On the night of the MTV Europe Music Awards in November 2004, about 117 million households across Europe tuned in to watch Beyoncé Knowles, Robbie Williams, and a glittering roster of other international celebrities parade under the klieg lights outside a massive tent on the outskirts of Edinburgh.

The continuing broad appeal of such events, almost two decades after MTV made its debut on this side of the Atlantic, gives testimony to the reach of the MTV brand here and to the apparently universal appeal of music videos, especially among the world's 14–29-year-olds.[4]

MTV's impact within the music industry is celebrated with its annual MTV Video Music Awards extravaganza shows held around the globe. The award shows are themselves a celebration of today's music in a global context.

When Edinburgh hosted the MTV Europe Music Awards ceremony in 2004, the Scottish economy was reportedly boosted by nearly £9 million. The show itself was beamed to viewers in 28 countries.[5] The attraction, excitement, visual appeal, and inspiration generated by these events add to the overall image of MTV as the leading, relevant, international, and up-to-date celebrant of today's music. Munich, in Germany, no doubt benefited in a similar way when it hosted the awards in 2007.

Providing a Personal Connection with Young People

MTV's youth culture-oriented content is the catalyst that provides the personal connection with young people. This is achieved through extensive research on trends and issues that are relevant and appealing to youth. The interactive nature of MTV's 360-degree convergent programming of TV, Internet, and mobile essentially delivers a heightened sense of participation and empowerment to the viewer.

Shows such as *TRL* allow viewers to vote online for their favorite videos through MTV.com. The multitude of musical genres on MTV Radio offers options to immediately download and purchase one's choice of music. This ongoing and consistent dialogue enables MTV to constantly churn out its message to its audience, wherever they are. The resulting sense of community, known as the "MTV Nation," ensures that the MTV brand rules.

Although MTV provides a window to the world on youth culture, determining the local implications is crucial in order to make the content relevant to its global audience. Locally tailored programming using local faces and local artists increases brand relevance to the respective audiences. Hence, the people factor looms large in this strategy, as audiovisual stimulants inadvertently affect human behavior and provide the personal connection. MTV's

VJs play a major role in achieving this effect. (See Chapter 8 for more about MTV's VJ strategy.)

The personalized aspect of MTV is manifested through its ethnographical eye on local youth culture. For instance, MTV's willingness to promote local bands within Southeast Asia on the channel has given birth to a new and interesting blend of Eastern-influenced sounds infused with modern hip-hop, called "Malay rap." Although few people believed that Malay rap would ever really take off in the music scene, groups such as Singaporean band Ahli Fiqir have confounded critics with hit songs such as "Samseng" and "Angguk-Angguk Geleng-Geleng," which are making waves with listeners in the region.

This global–local hybrid of Eastern and Western music has enabled MTV to penetrate into the Malay-speaking markets of Singapore, Malaysia, and Indonesia. Establishing this middle ground not only helps to expand MTV's viewer base, but also broadens the collective Malay-Muslim mindset while providing a platform for home-grown artists.

Expressing the Attitudes, Styles, and Interests of Today's Generation of Youth Culture

MTV's positioning as being the first and most authentic music television channel empowers creative freedom, which essentially engineers the buzz factor. The proactive strategy that entails willingness to break new ground recaptures the original MTV spirit, which in turn ensures the freshness of the brand. This competitive edge positions MTV as a leader in youth culture.

MTV's willingness to interact with its audience gives the channel unique insights into their lives, which are then built into its content. This customized approach creates an emotional connection with the viewer. Hence, the content is expanded to include practical issues relevant to viewers, which requires constant innovation and learning how to express the attitudes and styles of today's youth generation. Says Todd Cunningham, MTV senior vice president of strategy and planning:

> Before MTV even had ratings, a big part of what separated MTV from the pack of the other competitors out there was its knowledge of the audience and its mastery of understanding why an advertiser or why anyone who wanted to be affiliated with this brand would want to be there, because they understood the audience so well... So this is all about getting inside the texture of their lives...

MTV's pro-social initiative, *think* MTV, informs and empowers young people to take action on issues such as education, discrimination, the environment, sexual health, and global concerns. These "how-to" programs relate directly to the lives of young people and give them a foothold on pro-social causes that are close to their hearts. (See Chapter 8 for examples.)

The underlying fact is that the Millennial Generation is the most informed of all the generations, and they want to be heard. MTV reciprocates this characteristic of youth by giving them a voice and the opportunity to make a difference through volunteerism and such. This is in tandem with the forces of the "Relationship Age" that are exemplified by the Millennial Generation's need for self-expression. For example, MTV has teamed up with Youth Venture to enable young people to organize community efforts aimed at making a difference on a range of domestic and global issues. The thrust of the project is to offer grants of up to US$1,000 a week to teams of two or more young people to support such efforts.

Programs that are interactive and require risk-taking appeal to young people, who prefer to experience things for themselves and not be passive observers. MTV is always ahead of its competitors and in touch with its viewers because it isn't afraid of picking up on new trends.

The final aspect of MTV's positioning is its ability to be open and real with its viewers. The need to create relationships and build trust has never been more important, as young people are more discerning as a result of being overloaded with information. Hence, these factors augment MTV's global position of being totally devoted to young people.

The power of the MTV brand has resulted in the generation of several "brand equities" that have added to its market leadership and value.

TANGIBLE AND INTANGIBLE BRAND EQUITIES

Having built a powerful brand platform, MTV has gone on to build and acquire both tangible and intangible "equities" or properties that it "owns" and which help deliver the brand promise.

Tangible MTV Equities

Tangible brand equities are those assets of a brand that are largely visible. In the case of MTV, these are:

- informed, relatable VJs
- music video shows
- original animation
- lifestyle shows
- special events.

Informed, Relatable VJs

An important aspect of MTV's VJ requirements is that the person must be compelling on air and able to connect and engage with the audience. MTV VJs need to embody the MTV brand personality and values, as well as their own individual personalities. The qualities of being *relevant, passionate, unpredictable, clever, really funny, risk-taking, bold, open, and no bullshit.* may be manifested differently in terms of local culture, current global and local trends and fads, as well as viewers' lifestyles, opinions, and values. MTV has developed a strategy to have VJs who are as close to the target market as possible, in order to reflect relevant views and speak to the audience in a way they can relate to. (Again, for a more detailed discussion on VJs, see Chapter 8.)

Music Video Shows

The value of music videos has a lot to do with the power and influence of music in a young person's life. The visualization of music brings the viewer close to the artist, allowing him or her to perceive the artist's emotions and to receive directly the message intended for him or her. Pioneering artists of the music video phenomenon, such as Michael Jackson, experienced record sales of their albums. In fact, Jackson's 1984 *Thriller* album, which received repeated airplay on MTV, still holds the record for the highest number of sales. Tapping into this communicative aspect of music videos, MTV began creating music video shows that revolved around the viewer.

Original Animation

MTV's first animated series, *Beavis & Butt-Head*, which was aired from 1993 to 1997, was created around two IQ-challenged teenage boys whose lifestyles revolved around music videos, home, and school. The show highly influenced the vocabulary of American youth in the 1990s, through its subtle social criticisms as well as creative and intelligent comedy. *Daria*, a spin-off from *Beavis & Butt-Head*, was another popular series that aired from 1997 to 2001. *Daria* was an icon for the "teen misfit"—bespectacled, highly intelligent, and plainly dressed, unlike the typically trends-obsessed teenager. The "real-world," satirical nature of these animations, which were devoid of pretensions and the fantasy elements and "plasticity" associated with normal cartoon characters, appealed to the Millennials.

In 2000, MTV Asia launched LiLi, an animated, virtual VJ who interacted with viewers on air and online in five Asian languages. LiLi's responses were controlled by a person behind the image, allowing her to interview artists and provide information on pop culture to viewers. LiLi (no longer on the air) proved to be so popular with Asian teens that, prior to linking with Sony, Ericsson launched a line of LiLi mobile phones.

The fascination with animations is an extension of childhood experiences and emotions in youth. MTV's understanding of this particular need is given a mature twist so as not to talk down to its audience; instead, it reaches out to them with funny, often twisted depictions of their own lives. These original animations are testament to MTV's pioneering efforts in reaching out to all aspects of teen culture.

Lifestyle Shows

MTV pioneered the lifestyle or reality show with *Real World*. Most lifestyle shows highlight aspects of real life that relate to the viewer. Programmes such as *Newlyweds*, which featured Jessica Simpson and Nick Lachey, and *MTV Cribs* not only opened a window to the lifestyles of celebrities, but also allowed them to be human and accessible in the eyes of their fans. Shows such as *Pimp My Ride*, *Room Raiders*, and *Taildaters* offer practical tips on issues of life to which viewers can relate.

Recently introduced lifestyle shows include *8th & Ocean, Dancelife, Boiling Point, MTV's The 70s House, The Wade Robson Project*, and *Date My Mom*. Most of these programs are shown in the United States, but they occasionally find their way into Asian countries, as is the case with *Boiling Point*.

MTV Whatever Things (no longer on the air) gave Asian viewers a chance to win a contest to co-host the program, as well as to fly to New York to watch a live show at MTV Studios in Times Square featuring the most popular VJs and artists. At MTV Italy, stars appear in an on-the-set kitchen in the studio, catering to Italians' enjoyment of food. In India, audience appeal beckons toward national obsessions such as cricket and soap operas of the Bollywood genre, prompting MTV to order serials from India's top production company.

The aim of these programs is to reflect lifestyles to which the viewer can relate. For example, *The Osbournes* was completely alien to viewers in India, but is making waves among the more Westernized viewers of Southeast Asia. Ultimately, customization of content figures largely in tailoring lifestyle programs to suit the tastes of different viewers.

Special Events

MTV has about a dozen awards shows globally each year, roughly one a month; seven of these are in Asia alone. The shows are adaptations of the original annual MTV Video Music Awards, customized to suit MTV's local channels. Once again, the viewers rule the outcome by voting for their favorite videos and artists aired on MTV.

The MTV Asia Awards are a spectacular, much-anticipated event viewed right around the region. Over 16 million votes were cast in 2005, more than for any other MTV international award show. The event is a unique blend of East and West, with the largest gathering of international artists as well as artists from the region. It is also the only event that brings the youth of the region together in celebration of their music, from both local and regional perspectives. This is a remarkable feat in a region as diverse as Asia, which has long been divided and has never witnessed the coming together of its various peoples.

In 2005 the event was positioned as a global benefit in support of the victims of the 2004 Asian Tsunami. R&B diva Alicia Keys played host to more than 11,000 fans gathered to show their support for the cause. This in itself is testament to MTV's role as the voice of global youth, which is especially pertinent in this "Relationship Age."

Intangible MTV Equities

Intangible brand equities are those assets or properties that are not easily visible but which contribute a great deal to the success of the brand. In MTV's case, these are largely to do with content creation. While the output of content creation can be seen, it is the skill of creation and the depth of response of viewers that constitutes the intangible side.

In the world of branding, consumers value a product that resonates most with him or her. Hence, MTV's intangible equities have everything to do with content that is entertaining, enriching, and relevant for its audiences. As we have seen, MTV literally worships the consumer. This focus is reflected in its positioning statement—MTV is "totally devoted to young people through music, personal connections and a voice for youth culture"—and it delivers on this with its content creation.

Although certain resounding themes are common to youth all over the world, MTV recognizes that its viewers in 180 countries are decidedly diverse. There is a genuine need for MTV to customize content for different regions and countries, in a global–local strategy that gives it a highly international flavor as we have seen in this and earlier chapters.

International Content

The varied international content isn't the only thing that sets MTV apart from the competition. The differential factor is MTV's original content, which leverages the channel as an authority on music and youth culture. MTV's boldness in airing pioneering musical genres such as hip-hop and Malay rap has launched many musical careers. MTV's lifestyle programs, too, are a platform for trend spotting. *The Osbournes* showcased the psychographics prevalent in today's families—a world away from the family life depicted in shows of yesteryear such as *The Waltons*.

Variety: New, Informational, and with Visual Appeal

MTV's musical and lifestyle programs are tailored to draw the viewer closer. They not only celebrate the musical experience, but also encourage a personal connection with the viewer through the interactive nature of MTV. Shows such as *Becoming*, where viewers are selected to perform as the stars of their favorite music videos, truly provide the ultimate music experience for young people. *Becoming* was used to launch MTV Southeast Asia, where fans of Britney Spears were chosen to perform like her in a music video.

These upbeat and up-to-date shows are always a hit with MTV's audiences, not only for their informational and visual appeal, but also for the emotional connection that resonates with the viewer. MTV's informational and visually appealing lifestyle content, conveyed via the network's music and personal connections, enhances MTV's intangible equities.

Although MTV continues to be the voice of youth culture, no matter what language that voice may be speaking in, it always remains reflective of the hopes, fears, dreams, and desires of that voice. In January 2001, MTV went dark for 17 hours; during that time it scrolled through a list of the names of the many hundreds of people who have been victims of hate crimes in the United States. It was proof that when MTV wants to send out a message, it can do it even silently. Be it about HIV/AIDS, discrimination, or environmental degradation, when MTV adds its voice to the cause, the world hears, making it the world's foremost media brand.

The adage that MTV "understands me," as perceived by youth, holds true over time. Competitors fall short, and most are perceived as pale imitations of MTV's original programming and content ideas. MTV's first-to-the-market strategy is a result of the brand's wealth of both financial and non-financial resources, as well as experience. The MTV juggernaut, which currently encompasses over a billion viewers worldwide, has been ranked as the world's most valuable media brand with a brand value of US$6.647 billion.[6]

> Media moguls can babble on about the global village, about how CNN or BBC can reach out and touch the world. But those news shows are bush league operations compared to MTV's clout.[7]

This inescapable fact leads us to consider the emotional and rational benefits that the MTV faithful get from their brand, the place they go to and call their own.

The Sense of Belonging

The need to feel that one belongs, which is inherent in every human being, is heightened in adolescence when young people are trying to find their identities. Familiarity, rather than breeding contempt, is welcome; hence, familiar music, faces, and places are vitally important in creating a sense of security. On the other hand, as Jekyll is to Hyde, the fickleness and extreme emotions that are typical of youth cause them to yearn for excitement and self-expression. MTV, the home of youth culture, has succeeded in converging all these emotions, hopes, and dreams, and making young people feel important, boundless, real, and close to their heroes through a channel they can call their very own.

MTV's research efforts play a major part in understanding young people; what they are all about, how they think, and what their lives revolve around. This mastery of understanding and staying relevant to the viewer has been embraced and applied throughout the organization.

Although MTV makes use of traditional research methods—it has studied more than 200 focus groups—it is aware of the need to reinvent the wheel in order to stay fresh. Hence, it regularly conducts ethnographical studies, where researchers visit the homes of young people to study the way they live, their clothes, and their music collections, as well as studying trends and fads, young people's social interactions, be it in the home, at school, or in sporting or nightclub settings. The aim of this research is to understand the hearts and minds of young people: what matters most to them in terms of issues such as family, their peers, dating, and school; and their hopes and fears. These valuable consumer insights are then translated into programming opportunities to reflect what MTV's audience is all about.

The sense of belonging that draws viewers like a magnet is augmented by other benefits, as discussed below.

Always Relevant

The adherence to being relevant conveys a sense of belonging to the viewer when they see a reflection of their lives on MTV. The cogency of the message in the mindset of the viewer takes effect only when the issue at hand is of personal relevance to them. Thus,

MTV is spot-on when it tailors its content to convey a sense of belonging to its viewers through both tangible and intangible means, such as portraying people, places, things, and attitudes that young people identify with the most. Everything from the indoor studio set designs and outdoor location venues and events, to the VJs, celebrities, and fashion, as well as the issues addressed, pertain to young people.

The role of research and ethnographical studies became even more crucial as MTV grew to be a worldwide phenomenon. The channel initiated an 18-city worldwide study called "Sources of Gold" to find out what young people identified with the most in life, in an effort to understand their hearts and minds. The valuable data gathered enabled MTV to better understand the global marketplace. As a result, it was able to convey its familiar sense of belonging to its myriad global audiences through its pioneering, customized "glocal" strategy.

The localized content gives viewers a sense of far and the assurance that MTV values them enough to go lengths to accommodate their needs. As mentioned earlier, when MTV India incorporated Bollywood elements into its initial US-style content, its ratings soared. Understanding local intricacies forges an emotional link with the viewer that helps to build brand relevance and loyalty.

Discovery, Connection, and Attraction

Without a doubt, the nuances of the "Relationship Age" factor greatly in the dynamics of emotional and rational benefits for MTV's viewers. The Millennials, who make up the bulk of MTV's viewers, are incredibly media- and tech-savvy, and able to filter out messages that are irrelevant, unreal, and inauthentic, having been saturated with brands since they were in diapers. Hence, MTV needed to move on from mere attraction and entertainment through music, visuals, and styles by using the experiential elements of discovery and connection. Programs such *Stand In* on mtvU transmit the attraction by having celebrities such as Madonna,

Cameron Diaz, and Kanye West stand in as "professor for the day" at various American universities.

To counter skepticism and disloyalty among the Millennials, MTV has gone beyond just knowing about and making itself known to its audience; it reaches out and makes the connection by building trust among its viewers worldwide. The experiential extensions of the brand's 360-degree marketing approach not only inform viewers about current lifestyle aspirations but also establish vital two-way connectivity through the interactive features of the Internet and mobile technologies.

The 24/7 manner in which MTV reaches out to its audiences helps the brand go beyond the rational benefits to build the essential emotional capital required for brand loyalty. Viewers essentially trust MTV because the channel continuously innovates in order to keep the momentum of the relationship dynamics consistent.

A Channel of Expression and a Social Conscience

MTV's dedication to connecting to its audiences, not only through providing relevant content but also by being a channel of self-expression as well as a social conscience for the youth of the world, has been rewarded by the recognition of the brand as the voice of youth culture. "Passion, being honest and building relationships are attitudes that MTV has in its programming," said Alex Kuruvilla, MTV India's former managing director. "We view the tried and tested with suspicion. We celebrate the irreverent, the offbeat, and the sound of surprise."[8]

MTV gives youth just what it wants; it understands young people's moods, feelings, and insecurities, their need to say what they believe in and what they think is wrong, their "I'll live forever" attitude, and so much more.

SUMMARY OF EMOTIONAL AND RATIONAL VIEWER BENEFITS: "I BELONG HERE"

Like any great brand, MTV generates benefits for consumers that embody both rational and emotional elements. We have already seen that emotional benefits are the key to building brand relationships, and that MTV provides these. In sum, the brand satisfies the main drivers of youth needs and wants, and is really a place they call "home."

A place to call your own may be loud, funny, and unpredictable, but above all it must reflect your heart and soul. In effect, it is a place of unconditional acceptance. This sense of belonging is the "hot button" that MTV presses, and to which youth respond.

Figure 5.1 illustrates how youth use MTV, and music in particular, to gain a plethora of rational and emotional benefits.

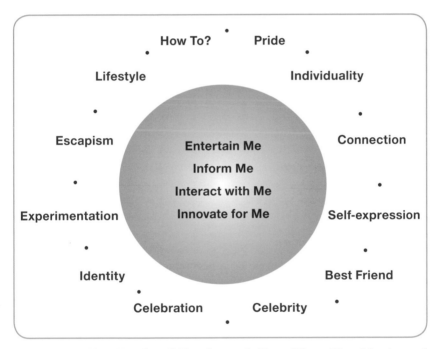

Figure 5.1 The Needs of Youth, and How They Use Music and MTV to Fulfill Them

Music is a safe way to take risks, as it gives youth a chance to experience other people going all the way to the edge in a virtual, but real, world. Younger viewers may want funky and exciting content, as in programs such as A*dvance Warning*, whereas older viewers may prefer more informative content as provided in *Wanna Come In?*, *Trippin'* and *MTV News*.

Whoever or whatever their preferences, MTV has something for everyone. The network manages to convey the benefits of entertainment, expression, and a sense of belonging to its viewers through music. The large variety of music genres available on the channel empowers youth to experiment, be creative, celebrate, and have a sense of pride in their various identities. MTV provides viewers with avenues for self-expression, escapism, and connection with the global world through its interactive mediums. More examples of how it does this can be seen in Chapter 8.

The fun doesn't stop there, as MTV not only allows viewers to get close to celebrities but also helps to make viewers' dreams come true by giving them a leg up on their road to achieving stardom. By providing all these opportunities, MTV builds powerful relationships with its viewers, who perceive it as a best friend who understands their needs. It's small wonder the brand has become a global icon.

In the next chapter you will read about some of the brand and business strategies that have taken MTV to the top.

1 MTV Brand Mission Statement, reproduced with permission of MTV.
2 Reproduced with permission of MTV.
3 Ibid.
4 Nicola Clark, "Competitors Struggle in Stagnant Market: Music Channels Fight for Ad Sales in Europe," *International Herald Tribune*, April 12, 2004, http://www.iht.com/articles/2004/04/12/musictv_ed3_.php.
5 Chris Heard, "Do We Still Want Our MTV?" *BBC News*, March 25, 2004, http://news.bbc.co.uk/2/hi/entertainment/3567155.stm.
6 "The 100 Top Brands 2006," *BusinessWeek*, July 28, 2006. http://bwnt.businessweek.com/brand/2006.
7 "MTV's World: Mando-Pop. Mexican Hip Hop. Russian Rap. It's all fueling the biggest global channel," *BusinessWeek*, February 18, 2002, http://www.businessweek.com/magazine/content/02_07/b3770009.htm.
8 Menka Shivadasani, "The Coolest Trends," Business Line, *Financial Daily*, July 23, 2001.

MTV Shows
Be on MTV
Live Performances
Genres
Shop MTV Shows
Europe Music Awards
MTV Shows Gossip
Show Photos
Shop

6

The MTV Brand and Business Strategies

In looking at MTV's brand and business strategies, we can see some very specific areas where MTV has succeeded in gaining a sustainable competitive advantage, namely:

- the drive for globalization
- digitalization
- localization strategy
- the deliberate non-export of MTV's US heritage
- innovation

- brand and line extensions
- "niching" and category segmentation
- joint ventures
- cross-selling: advergaming
- living the brand: passion and the MTV people.

We will now examine each of these advantages in turn.

THE DRIVE FOR GLOBALIZATION:
MTV—THE ESPERANTO OF GLOBAL YOUTH CULTURE

> Esperanto is the most widely spoken constructed international auxiliary language. Esperanto is culturally neutral by design as it was intended to be a facilitator between cultures, not the carrier of any one national culture.[1]

In relation to the above, it wouldn't be too far off the mark to say that MTV is the Esperanto of global youth culture. The channel is ubiquitous worldwide with its localized versions of MTV, yet its personality, which is without a country of origin, can be easily recognized. MTV Networks CEO Judy McGrath was quoted as saying, "We just finished another plan ... and international is in the DNA of every sentence."[2]

MTV's presence in 164 countries and 18 languages, with 100 channels reaching around a billion viewers globally,[3] makes it a truly international brand. The number of viewers is expected to increase to 2.8 billion by the year 2010, and they will have the means to purchase CDs, jeans, and whatever brands are young and hip. It is for these demographic and psychographic reasons that international brands love MTV International. The attitude, feel, and unique quirkiness of the interstitials that is distinctly MTV helps to maintain the consistency of the brand internationally.

MTV beams several global shows worldwide, including *TRL* and special events such as the MTV Video Music Awards, to keep its viewers worldwide updated on the global music scene. MTV gives its global audience the opportunity through contests to attend such events and celebrate today's music experience. MTV's global presence has also given local musicians international exposure, through appearing on regional stations and performing at the network's international events. For instance, Senegalese artist Akon was featured live on MTV's *Nokia Unwired at Hard Rock Live* in Orlando, Florida. The international nature of the network helps spread the various musical genres all over the globe.

The international personality of the MTV brand is not only present in its music shows but is also portrayed via its lifestyle shows and special events. Programs with an international appeal include *TRL*, *My Super Sweet 16*, *Hip Hop Countdown*, *Celebrity Deathmatch*, and *I Want a Famous Face*.

Above all, MTV's international personality is projected through its worldwide social concerns, such as HIV/AIDS, diversity, and global poverty. Incidentally, Bill Roedy is a UNAIDS ambassador and a former chair of the Global Business Coalition on HIV/AIDS, a United Nations partner organization. This is testament to MTV's international outreach and to its position as representing the universal voice of youth culture. MTV has leveraged this position to get its social messages to millions of its viewers, who are essentially the youth of the world. In this respect, MTV is the Esperanto of global youth culture.

DIGITALIZATION

In the 1980s, MTV spurred on the digital revolution and its acute perception of its viewers' preferences. MTV provides artists with instant recognition, because of the wide scope of its exposure. Today, MTV aims to drive its content not only laterally to the outer corners of the world, but also vertically so that no one is left out.

The broadband video channel MTV Overdrive was launched in April 2005 to deliver the network's content to viewers everywhere they demand it: on-air, online, via wireless, video-on-demand, and more. The service includes six separate channels of programming with highlights of the day's programming, such as music, news, and film trailers; exclusive, four-times-a-day news updates; behind-the-scenes access to original MTV television programming; a movie channel, including film trailers and celebrity interviews; personal style; and, needless to say, sufficient music to keep the viewers happy. Videogame culture will be incorporated in the near future. In addition to the United States, MTV Overdrive is available in Brazil, Italy, and the Netherlands, among other countries. "Like our audience, we are always evolving, finding new ways to create compelling content for breakthrough technologies, and Overdrive is a powerful new platform that allows users to have more control over the way they experience MTV," Van Toffler, MTV Network's group president, has been quoted as saying.[4]

Product innovation liberates MTV's content from the traditional restricted television platform to reach out to its audiences through new channels. For example, MTV's adaptation of the digital revolution to provide content via a joint venture with mobile phone giant Motorola will have a sweeping effect on global youth. This "Mobile TV" is another landmark first for MTV. A further feather in MTV's digital cap is its collaboration with Microsoft to provide content via the latter's Xbox 360 game console. Toffler explains: "Our audiences want to connect with our content on every platform they interact with—linear television, broadband, online, radio and now on PCs ... that helps fulfill our multiplatform entertainment promise ... to take the entire entertainment experience to the next level."

LOCALIZATION STRATEGY

In linguistics, "agglutination" is the morphological process of adding affixes to the base word.[5] The global organic growth of MTV has adopted a similar agglutinant approach by adding local flavors to its core brand values to make MTV meaningful to its viewers wherever in the world they may be. The key is to be relevant and relatable, as well as to create a sense of belonging by using faces, music, and places that are familiar to audiences in every outpost of MTV without changing its core values.

The advent of globalization heralded changes in social orders and economies around the world. The dramatic increase in international trade and the falling of trade barriers, coupled with cross-cultural exchanges, have meant that many markets have become homogenized. Nevertheless, the variations between countries and cultures highlight the necessity for customized approaches. Cultures around the globe are markedly different in terms of language, societal organizations, dress, traditions, shared moral values, environmental interactions, and religions. The sum of it is that one size doesn't fit all.

Many companies have fallen along the wayside, or been seen as cultural imperialists, while trying to export their brand culture. A desirable model would be a brand that is consistent with central values, yet which could be adapted to a local context. Essentially, local variations incorporated into the global premise make the brand more meaningful and relatable to a person wherever in the world they may be. Bill Roedy, president of MTV Networks International, made the comment:

> The other strand of MTV's marketing strategy is localization. ... These are tailored not only to reflect cultural and linguistic differences, but increasingly, variations in musical taste. The wonders of digital technology are allowing MTV to create channels for those who like rock, rap, techno, and so on. But remember—although you can adjust the content, it is essential that you maintain the brand's values. MTV means "irreverent," *Vogue* means "elegant," the *FT* means "business." Lose sight of your core message and you could lose control of your brand.

In view of this, MTV seems to have mastered the art of "glocalization" with its successful formula of integrating local tastes with global youth culture so as to avoid charges of being a cultural imperialist. It is a matter of understanding the global target audience and what viewers in India, China, Southeast Asia, Europe, or the United States want, which will vary immensely in every context. This dichotomy is reflected in the ratio of global–local content in each of MTV's local or regional stations. Local content outweighs the international content for audiences in India and China, where there are strong sentiments about local language and culture. (See Chapter 10 for detailed case studies on MTV China and MTV India.)

Global versus Local Content

The goal of MTV's localization programming is to have almost 70% local content. Thus, the build-up requires a long-term commitment. In Southeast Asia, especially in Singapore and Malaysia, global content outweighs the local. This is due both to the region's long exposure to Western culture and the English language, and to the dearth of a vibrant local music scene as a result of the paternal nature of those countries' governments. The melting pot of cultures in Singapore and Malaysia also seems to justify this strategy of using American/European music and shows such as *TRL* and *Pimp My Ride*. MTV has also been reaching out to the young people of Asia by holding localized versions of its events and shows, such as *Boiling Points—Malaysia Edition*.

Local Talent

MTV has become so adept at global–local strategies that it was no surprise that its 100th channel, MTV Base, began broadcasting in Africa early in 2005, bringing popular music back to its roots, which lie in the rhythms of Africa. MTV's localized strategy also has a global agenda, which is to showcase talents from the African music industry on its worldwide stage. The channel is optimistic

about the global acceptance of distinctly African musical genres such as "kwaito" and the Zulu form of hip-hop. On the occasion of the launch of the new channel, Bill Roedy said: "The stars are aligned. You've got a great gig here." Roedy commented that most music has its roots in Africa, and described the continent as "a source of cool."[6]

This strategy of bringing local music out of obscurity and into the global limelight has popularized groups such as Taiwan's Jay Chou and Jolin Tsai, the Russian female duet group Tatu, and Colombia's Shakira. Jay Chou's popularity in Asia has even caught the attention of Irish boy band Blue, and rumors of a potential collaboration have spread. Most of these talents have been discovered as the result of foraging in local markets by MTV's local executives and VJs.

Apart from local artists and signature content, MTV has a knack of creating unique individual personalities at its local channels who relate to local viewers. Carson Daly of the United States, Cyrus Broacha in India, and Utt and Denise Keller in Southeast Asia embody in their own personalities the global brand values of MTV, such as "irreverent," "whacky," "funny," "clever," and "youthful," and express them through local peculiarities.

Local Empowerment

Ultimately, MTV's local programmers are empowered to decide on the content mix for their own channels. This editorial independence is important, as local programmers are most aware of what is entertaining, enriching, and relevant for their audiences and thereby able to deliver the appropriate content for the targeted audience.

Although MTV, as the "voice of youth," has been instrumental in globalizing the youth of the world through its universal youth culture, it always emphasizes local voices, which is what endears it to its viewers around the world. This is a very different approach than just exporting American youth culture. Needless to say, advertisers—both global and local—are more than happy with

MTV's outreach, which currently stands at a global audience of over a billion.

The editorial independence of local programmers encourages creativity, integrity, diversity, and quality, and mirrors MTV's "glocal" strategy. MTV's celebration of the diversity of its viewers, eight out of ten of whom live outside the United States, communicates that the channel is not all about exporting American youth culture to the world. However, the channel is receptive to the fact that although international viewers want a staple of local music, they also want to connect to the world at large and keep abreast of global music and youth culture. Thus, the "glocal" mix varies from market to market, with individual content tailored to suit local audiences' musical tastes, humor, and values.

At the end of the day, it is experience that makes the difference, because MTV's activities must be accretive and profitable to ensure shareholders a return on their investments. Market strategies are thoroughly planned through intensive target market research within each of MTV's localization strategies. Expensive non-music productions that deviate from MTV's music-based youth culture fast lose appeal among the target audiences and make it hard to garner advertising revenue. Hence, a natural balance is needed between creative ideas and commercial viability. Once again, this reiterates that MTV's localization strategy centers on the winning formula of combining universal youth culture with local flavors.

Think Local, Not USA: "Customize" is the Name of the Game

It would have been extremely tempting for MTV to export US culture via its heritage, but it has deliberately chosen not to do so. As Bill Roedy commented: "MTV is not an exporter of American culture. And we are not in the business of steamrolling Anglo-American music on the world. How could we? Eight out of 10 MTV viewers are outside of the US. We were local before local was cool."

MTV focuses on the needs and values of its audiences, wherever they may hail from. MTV's localization strategy drives growth, ratings, and revenue, because essentially the channel worships the consumer by putting their needs and wants first. MTV's 100 individual channels mirror the diversity of the network's viewers.

Having been the voice of youth for almost a quarter of a century, MTV not only knows what its audiences want, but also how to deliver it to them. Although young people want to connect to a whole world of music and youth culture, local music is indispensable. Hence, the ideal "glocalization" blend envisioned by MTV for all its channels would be 70% local and 30% global content. This formula is customized according to individual market variables. Bill Roedy again:

> The best example of customization is our MTV awards shows. We now have a dozen awards shows globally—seven right here in Asia—including two in Mainland China, and an event each in Singapore, Taiwan, the Philippines, Indonesia, and Japan. We have awards for everyone. While featuring international artists and the MTV vibe, each show is tailored to suit local audiences' musical tastes, humor and values... Each one is totally unique... The MTV Asia Awards ... is a magical blend of East meets West like no other MTV show.

The crux of MTV's localization is to reflect the local culture to the world, while having its viewers chant the network's clarion call, "I want my MTV," in Russian or Mandarin, because MTV reflects their national identity, hopes, dreams, and desires back at them.

INNOVATION

Just as Madonna displays a promotional genius for reinventing herself, MTV's success revolves primarily around capturing the essence and maintaining the freshness of the brand. Hence, content has always been the heartbeat of MTV's innovative brilliance.

By the mid-1980s, changes to MTV's content were imminent because the basic visual radio format had become predictable, causing the freshness factor to be diminished. In order to remain relevant to its audience, MTV's team of creative geniuses has produced some of television's best entertainment, such as hit animated social satires *Beavis & Butt-Head* and *Daria*. Pioneering reality shows included *Real World* and the notorious family series *The Osbournes*. Other successful formats included the uproarious prank show *Punk'd* and stunt show *Jackass*, as well as highly successful global entertainment events such as the MTV Video Music Awards.

Interstitials, or animation shorts such as "Bad Logo" that serve as creative fillers between programs, allude to the innovative nature of MTV. "Bad Logo" is an uncouth and unwelcome visitor that has an MTV logo for a head; "Mr. Viril" is an oddball character who has a thing for sadistic women; and "Happy Tree Friends" indirectly exemplifies the irreverent and risk-taking theme of the MTV brand. MTV communicates to its attention span-challenged viewers through deft editing skills and brazen imagery.

Going a step further in the learning curve of youth culture, MTV has been at the forefront of taking on youth-related topics such as sexual health, racism, and drugs, as well as national and global issues. MTV uses music as the basis for communicating with viewers about social and environmental issues, as well as the changes that are taking place in the world. For instance, as stated earlier, the 2005 MTV Asia Awards were used to raise funds for the 2004 Asian Tsunami victims. Hence, viewers remain at the heart of MTV, which never talks down to its audiences yet maintains its core values of being relevant, passionate, unpredictable, clever, humorous, risk-taking, and bold.

The key is to remain relevant to each generation, and to stay on the creative edge of creating significant programming. MTV's research and creative foresight have been responsible for discovering and popularizing new musical genres. In the late 1980s and into the 1990s, for example, MTV brought hip-hop culture to the forefront through its groundbreaking program, *Yo! MTV Raps*. Likewise, boy bands such as 'N Sync and divas Britney

Spears and Christina Aguilera owe the success of their musical genres to MTV.

Although technology is part of MTV's innovative strategy, the fundamentals that have become the hallmark of the brand are content and creativity. Technology will always change, but it will never overcome the fundamental principle that content is king. By constantly looking for new talents and keeping abreast of upcoming trends in the music industry, as well as youth culture as a whole, MTV differentiates itself from its competitors by striving to be the best that it can be for its audience. Today, MTV's innovative relevancy is driving it to be as close as possible to its audiences on a 24/7 basis via its 360-degree marketing approach.

The interactive link is vital in the worldview of the Millennials, which is a continuous gamut of entertainment, information, and communication. This is especially effective in the conservative and private societies of Asia, where overt rebelliousness is frowned upon. The privacy of mobile phones allows Asian youth to express themselves through downloading customized ringtones and MTV logos.

MTV not only makes its content available to viewers online and via mobile telecommunications, but viewers also get to vote for their favorite choices during the MTV Video Music Awards and VJ Hunts. Collaborations with credit card companies such as Citibank in India and UOB in Singapore help to leverage further the MTV brand with its core demographic by alluring users to get discounts on merchandise, music, nightclubs, movies, and events such as the MTV Video Music Awards.

Going all out in its passion for music and innovation, as well as making its presence felt internationally and locally, plus digging deep to stay in touch with its audiences, describes the essence of MTV's brand drivers.

BRAND AND LINE EXTENSIONS

In addition to MTV, MTV Networks' television brand and line extensions include MTV2, VH1, mtvU, Nickelodeon, NICK at Nite,

SPIKE, Logo, Game One, Comedy Central, TV Land, CMT, Noggin, MTV Flux, MTV Networks International, The Digital Suite from MTV Networks, QOOB, Paramount Comedy, The N, TMF: The Music Factory, and VIVA. Its other entertainment brands include 365gay.com, afterellen.com, afterelton.com, Atom Entertainment, Gametrailers.com, GoCityKids.com, Neopets.com, Xfire.com, Y2M.com, ParentsConnect.com, MHD (Music High Definition) and Harmonix Music Systems.

MTV Networks' brands are seen in 496.1 million households in 162 countries and in 32 languages via 136 locally programmed and operated television channels and 137 websites.[7]

MTV Networks connects with its audiences through its robust consumer products businesses and its more than 80 interactive properties worldwide, including online, broadband, wireless, and interactive television services. It also has licensing agreements, joint ventures, and syndication deals, enabling all of its programming services to be seen worldwide.

Nickelodeon and VH1 are part of MTV's integrated branding strategy aimed at maintaining brand loyalty through a "cradle to grave"-type strategy. Nickelodeon was created as a precursor to MTV, and VH1 was aimed at those who had outgrown the MTV network. The fragmentation of the network was necessary, especially in the

> VH1 posted 2004 as its most-watched year ever in its 19-year history in both primetime and total day. Such original series as *Best Week Ever, I Love the '90s* and *My Coolest Years* helped the pop culture cabler score a double-digit gain among total viewers in total day, up 12% over last year. VH1 is also off to a strong start in 2005 with *The Surreal Life 4, Strange Love*, starring Flavor Flav and Brigitte Nielsen, and *Celebrity Fit Club*, all ranking as VH1's highest-rated series premieres of all time among 18–49s.[8]

case of VH1, in order to maintain both the freshness of the brand and its relevance to its target audience. One could not risk the scenario of having both children and parents watching the parents' favorite genre of music on a channel that was supposed to cater for the former. Hence, VH1's target audience is among the more mature Generation X-ers who are over 25 years of age.

Nickelodeon, on the other hand, was created to usher in MTV's future audiences based on the rationale that brand loyalties that are made in childhood remain for life. Incidentally, Nickelodeon's viewers are the tail end of the Millennials, whose infatuation with technology and designer brands is literally forged during infancy. The advantage of this integrated branding strategy is that MTV is guaranteed of the brand loyalty of its viewers for life, and their full potential will only be realized when the Nickelodeon children grow into MTV teens, who in turn will mature into VH1 consumers.

With a population of over 3.2 billion in 2002, and projected to grow to 5.6 billion in 2050, nearly half of whom are below the age of 35, the demographics make Asia the most fertile ground for the full potential of MTV's integrated brand strategy. Apart from MTV, MTV Networks Asia broadcasts twenty 24-hour Nickelodeon and VH1 branded channels in Asia-Pacific. Nickelodeon reaches over 171 million TV households in the region with channels and programming blocks, including six 24-hour channels—Nickelodeon Asia, Nickelodeon India, Nickelodeon Philippines, Nickelodeon Japan, and Nickelodeon and Nick Jr. Australia.

VH1 reaches approximately 20 million TV households in the region via four 24-hour services in Indonesia, India, Thailand, and Australia, as well as daily programming blocks on MTV Southeast Asia and MTV Philippines channels. Hence, one cannot but conclude that the sun is only just rising on MTV Asia's integrated branding strategy. Nickelodeon is a key part of that strategy.

Nickelodeon: Linking Age Segments for Onward Growth

Too young to be grown-ups and too old to be children; this is the psyche of today's tweens—aged between eight and 14—who make up the core of Nickelodeon's viewers. These sophisticated children are extremely self-reliant and think of themselves as friendly, happy, and smart, on top of being extremely tech- and brand-savvy.

Tween surveys in the United States reveal that this target market has been known to consume approximately seven hours of media a day, including television, videos, movies, music, computers, videogames, books, magazines, and newspapers—in addition to any media used in school or to complete homework. Television rates highly, with an average of six hours of kids' programs watched each week. In an average day, they spend 59 minutes reading a book, 52 minutes using a home computer, and 45 minutes playing videogames. Eighty percent of 12- to 14-year-olds and 75% of nine- to 12-year-olds watch music videos. Many of them go on to watch MTV in their teenage years.[9]

The integrated branding of Nickelodeon and MTV only makes sense because most of the former's target market would naturally progress on to the latter. The fragmentation of Nickelodeon's target market makes it a natural feeder that creates brand loyalty for MTV. Nick Jr. targets an audience of toddlers and preschoolers aged between two and five years, while TEENick is aimed at tweens up to 14 years. Nickelodeon's latest launch on the broadband platform, TurboNick on Nick.com, comes in a full-length series via the Internet. Part of its programming format includes Nicksclusives, featuring movie trailers, music videos, celebrity interviews, and game demonstrations that literally translate to a passport into the entertainment world of MTV.

Incidentally, viewers of Nickelodeon are termed the "Nickelodeon Nation," as the network recognizes them as an "influential market"[10] because of the considerable influence they wield over family purchases.

Nickelodeon has also launched a lifestyle-targeted digital cable network, GAS (the games and sports channel) and Noggin (an educational channel). Hence, Nickelodeon is creating an emotional connection with its viewers in a similar vein to MTV's 360-degree marketing approach. This "cradle to grave" strategy, whereby viewers begin with Nickelodeon and progress on to MTV and finally settle down with VH1 in later years, bringing their brand loyalty with them, translates into tangible financial value for advertisers. Drs. Elizabeth Preston and Cindy L. White, of Westfield State College, Massachusetts and Central Connecticut State University, respectively, commented in their article "Commodifying Kids: Branded Identities and the Selling of Adspace on Kids' Networks"[11] that Nickelodeon is an industry leader: "Nickelodeon owns 56% of all K6–11 Gross Rating Points in kids' commercial TV."

MTV is the pioneer of lifestyle branding, reaching out to its viewers in every aspect of their lives, and Nickelodeon has emulated a similar strategy; hence, MTV and Nickelodeon exemplify an "integrated branding network."[12]

Nickelodeon, which was first launched in the United States in 1979, is the world's only multimedia entertainment brand dedicated exclusively to children. It consists of 28 channels, 21 branded program blocks, and two broadband services available across Africa, Asia and the Pacific Rim, former Soviet Union, Europe, Latin America, and the United States. Nickelodeon is a one-stop entertainment brand for children with its innovative and original, curriculum-based, fun and commercial-free programs. Nick Jr. has won Emmy, Peabody, and Parents' Choice awards.

In a similar way to MTV, Nickelodeon has built a diverse, global business by putting its viewers first in everything it does. Nickelodeon's US television network is seen in 89 million households and has been the top-rated basic cable network for 10 consecutive years. The company also includes consumer products, online content, recreation, books, magazines, and feature films. Nickelodeon's programs, such as *Dora the Explorer* and *SpongeBob SquarePants*, remain television's most highly rated children's shows both in the United States and around the world. *SpongeBob SquarePants* has courted controversy by displaying homosexual leanings, thus alluding to the MTV brand personality of being bold and realistic in today's world; and yet "SpongeBob," as he is affectionately known, has become a global brand in "his" own right.

"Dora" has made a mark by being an iconic character in the Hispanic world because "she" breaks away from stereotypical depictions of a particular group of people. The popularity of the series has spawned a spin-off entitled *Go, Diego, Go!* Eight-year-old Diego, a bilingual animal rescuer and nature expert who has the ability to talk to animals, takes preschoolers on interactive, high-stakes journeys inspired both by the rich environments of Latin America and by the animals that make their homes in those habitats. In each episode, Diego and his friends encourage children to use scientific thinking and investigative strategies to help animals in trouble.

Other hit programs include TEENick features *Ned's Declassified School Survival Guide* and *Unfabulous*. Similar to MTV, Nickelodeon's brand experience extends to signature events such as its Kids' Choice Awards show, which has been expanded to its seven fully localized networks around the world. Herb Scannell, former vice chairman of MTV Networks and president of Nickelodeon Networks, comments:

> Nickelodeon's unifying global mission is to serve kids and put them first in all that we do. The network celebrated another milestone in June 2005 when Nickelodeon US, powered by shows such as *SpongeBob SquarePants, Zoey 101, The Fairly OddParents* and *Avatar*, recorded its 10th consecutive year as the number-one cable network on a total day basis, according to research company A. C. Nielsen.

MTV and Nickelodeon mirror each other in terms of their brand strategies of being totally devoted to young people and children through their signature branding experience.

"NICHING" AND CATEGORY SEGMENTATION

It was quite obvious that MTV's initial visual radio format would become predictable and stale within a few years if the network had not been receptive to new musical genres and lifestyle programming. This led to the rise of hip-hop in the late 1980s and early 1990s, when MTV popularized the genre with a new segment, *Yo! MTV Raps.*

Pop culture has always been the mainstay of MTV, but to satisfy the hard-core fans of the old-school visual radio MTV, the network spawned MTV2, a new channel with a mixed play list of hip-hop and rock 'n' roll. MTV2 caters for serious music aficionados and is devoid of teenybopper popular culture.

mtvU was also created for a niche audience of college students, and the network is aired on campuses across the United States. Logo is a new channel specially created for MTV's gay, lesbian, bisexual, and transgender viewers aged 25–49, whereas SPIKE is a gender-specific channel that caters to male audiences aged 18–49. NICK at Nite targets an audience aged 25–54 that stays up later at night and wants shows that are family-friendly, funny, and familiar.

The fact that MTV Networks recognizes that such niches and categories exist among its viewers is testament to the fact that the network really listens to and understands its audiences, which reiterates its claim to be "the voice of global youth culture." Sumner Redstone, chairman and CEO of Viacom, said in 2004:

> Take MTV. They do an enormous amount of research and have to be ready for each new generation. Each generation produces change. So far, they've been very successful in creating the kind of programming that each generation wants. They know they have to stay on the creative edge. They have, and that is the reason for their success.[13]

JOINT VENTURES

MTV's most prolific joint venture is in China with China Central Television (CCTV), the state-run television network through which MTV airs its programs. Another is with Shanghai Media Group, which produces Chinese content for MTV, including educational and children's programming. (See Chapter 10 for an in-depth look at MTV in China.)

CROSS-SELLING: ADVERGAMING

MTV's cross-selling strategies extend to product development in the area of gaming. This is a step away from traditional music-based programs, but the potential for this new product segment is immense. In 2003, MTV Networks International acquired a 50% stake in the French videogame cable channel Game One, marking MTV's inauguration into the gaming segment. In order to broaden its appeal, as well as to keep in line with MTV's youthful audience preferences for gaming, the network not only features games but also introduces new gaming products MTV-style.

In 2005 MTV acquired Neopets.com,[14] an online world of "virtual pets," founded in 1999 by two British students, Adam Powell and Donna Williams. The site, which now operates in 10 languages, has more than 30 million global users, more than 7 billion page views per month, and is one of the world's largest, stickiest, and fastest-growing sites among youth. Neopets' users "adopt" mythical pets that live in an alternative world called Neopia that has its own geography, pet species, and games. Users get to play interactive games, exchange messages, and submit stories, poems, and comics.

Site users range from 13 to 17 years old, with about 57% being female. Female audiences are likely attracted to the messaging and storytelling functions of the site. Most of the site's revenue comes from advertising, and it operates with a fairly small staff, making it extremely profitable. According to reports, MTV plans to expand the brand offline into television, movies, and publishing.

LIVING THE BRAND: PASSION AND THE MTV PEOPLE

MTV and its people exude passion and brand thinking. This passion for music and visual creation is a critical success factor for the MTV brand.

"After silence, that which comes nearest to expressing the inexpressible is music," wrote Aldous Huxley. Henry Wadsworth Longfellow expressed a similar sentiment when he described music as "the universal language of mankind." Music has always been a unifying force, a universal language that connects people, cultures, and ideas. Hence, it comes as no surprise that music is the Esperanto for universal youth culture. It is used by young people worldwide as a tool for talking to the mainstream of any society.

The surest way to penetrate the mindset of youth, whoever or wherever they may be, is to listen to their music. The MTV people have energy, passion, and an uncanny ability to understand the psyche of youth, even though some of them are no longer young! They do their homework through market research and by getting out on the streets, and, they then think hard about program content. MTV is the international dictionary for the universal language of youth.

MTV communicates effectively with its audiences by speaking their language. Music, especially popular music, is MTV's agglutinant, which has morphed into various forms across the globe. Songs are brought to life through the visualization and dramatization of the lyrics. The acting and dancing are usually performed by the artists themselves, or in some cases, by actors who dramatize the lyrics. The meaningful depiction of the storyline in music videos was such a phenomenon in the early 1980s that they were described as a new art form that dealt with controversial subject matter such as sex, violence, and other sensitive topics.

Artists such as Madonna, whose video "Papa Don't Preach" was about teen pregnancy, and Michael Jackson, whose "Billy Jean" was about fathering a child out of wedlock, thrived on these controversies. The lesbian Russian duo Tatu (the name is Russian slang for "This girl (loves) that girl") is another case in point. Tatu's video about same sex love, "I Lost My Mind," was voted by MTV Russia's viewers as the number one video of 2001, as well as making waves across the globe.

MTV not only brings music to life for its viewers, but also makes it relevant to them by being bold and risk-taking enough to allow their thoughts and feelings to be expressed on air. This creates a sense of belonging and the emotional connection between MTV and its audience. Hence, music videos of global artists form the basis for MTV's global brand drivers.

Universally popular shows such as *Pimp My Ride, TRL*, and *My Super Sweet 16* reinforce this phenomenon. MTV allows the viewer to celebrate the global music experience by connecting them to the channel directly, music celebrities, and fellow viewers across the globe via its 360-degree marketing approach. The personal connection that the network offers its viewers fuels their passion for music and confronts them with fresh, relevant, bold, risk-taking elements of music-based entertainment that is uniquely MTV. Even the staff display a natural passion for music. "Without music, MTV is just TV," said Guy Holmes, chairman of Gut Records.

MTV harnesses the power of music coupled with sensory information to capture the emotions of young people. "Campus Invasion 2K2," an interactive music expo and mobile promotional campaign by MTV, was held on 20 university campuses in the United States in April 2002. The network created a musical theme park where students were able to add their vocals to their favorite music tracks, add instruments, and perform on stage. They were given a customized CD and photograph of their performance to take home, along with their memories of forming an emotional connection with MTV from the experience.

MTV's passion for music is also exemplified in its efforts to promote new artists. For example, *Advanced Warning* is the network's collaboration with McDonald's to introduce emerging artists in a fresh format. The program was launched in the United States and has helped to launch the careers of various artists, including Joss Stone, Kanye West, Franz Ferdinand, and Maroon 5, all of whom have since achieved worldwide fame as well as Grammy nominations. The program has since expanded to Latin America and Asia. In 2005, *Advanced Warning* featured "5 in 05" as a fresh addition to the program, highlighting the five artists whom MTV believed would be most successful in that year. Jonathan Patrick, executive vice president of MTV Networks International Marketing Partnerships, Viacom, said in February 2005:

> *MTV Advance Warning* going global, in partnership with McDonald's, will enable MTV's audiences to be the first to see and hear the artists that we believe have the potential to achieve international success in 2005. By localizing *MTV Advance Warning*, we will be able to support these artists in a creative, relevant way that truly connects with our viewers.

The relentless exposure that successful entrants get by being featured on MTV is an instant passport to fame, courtesy of the network. MTV's passion for music turns regular people into superstars. Undeniably, music is the unifying factor that connects the "MTV Nation."

This chapter has examined how the MTV brand is delivered through various strategies. Chapter 7 analyzes further the factors that account for the competitive success of the brand.

1   *Wikipedia,* http://en.wikipedia.org/wiki/Esperanto.
2   Johnnie L, Roberts. "World Tour," *Newsweek,* June 6, 2005.
3   "McGrath transforms television., *CNN.com"*
     http://www.cnn.com/SPECIALS/2004/global.influentials/stories/
     mcgrath.profile.
4   Quoted in Jennifer LeClaire, "MTV Puts Music Videos into Overdrive,"
     TechNewsWorld, http://www.macnewsworld.com/story/42111.html.
5   *Wikipedia,* http://en.wikipedia.org/wiki/Agglutination.
6   Adele Shevel, "MTV Takes on Africa," *Sunday Times* (Johannesburg),
     February 27, 2005.
7   MTV Networks International Global Fact Sheet, December 5, 2006.
8   Viacom Inc: Company View, *www.cbronline.com,*
     http://www.cbronline.com/companyprofile.asp?guid=68021BD5-5AAC-42A5-
     B437-11958F2E0AB9&CType=View.
9   Statistics derived from "Popular Culture & the American Child," *Issue Brief*
     Series, (Studio City, CA: Mediascope Press, 1999).
10   Dr. Elizabeth Preston and Dr. Cindy L. White, "Commodifying Kids: Branded
     Identities and the Selling of Adspace on Kids' Networks," *Communication,*
     52 no. 2, (Spring) 2004.
11   Ibid.
12   J. Turow, *Breaking Up America: Advertisers and the New Media World,*
     Chicago: University of Chicago Press, (1997), quoted in Preston and
     White, ibid.
13   "The King of Content." Interview with Summer M. Redstone, *Outlook Journal,*
     June 2004, http://www.accenture.com/Global/Research_and_In
     sights/Outlook/By_Alphabet/TheKingOfContent.htm.
14   Dinesh C. Sharma, "MTV Acquires Virtual Critter Site NeoPets"
     CNET News.com, June 20, 2005, http://news.com.com/MTV+acquires+virtual
     +critter+site+NeoPets/2100-1030_3-5753858.html.

Music Videos Be on MTV
Live Performances Genres
Shop MTV Shows Show Photos
Europe Music Awards MTV Shows Gossip
Vid
Shop

7

Competitive Analysis and Brand Development

KEY FACTORS FOR COMPETITIVE SUCCESS

"MTV is the world's largest television network and the leading multimedia brand for youth. It is also Asia's Most Watched Music Channel in Asia Pacific, viewed by more young adults than any other music channel."[1] In 2004, MTV was named the "World's Most Valuable Media Brand" for the fifth consecutive year, and in 2006 *BusinessWeek* ranked it in the top 50 of the world's most valuable brands overall, with a value of US$6.627 billion.[2] In 2007, the MTV brand was valued at US$6.907 billion.[3]

The key factor for competitive success is how a company differentiates itself by a specialized stream of activity that is superior to or devoid in its competitors. Sustainable competitive advantage is attained via the long-term advantages of the company's core competencies. These success features encompass the company's ability to penetrate markets via its positive brand image, as well as the perceived customer benefits, which make it difficult for competitors to imitate.

The key factor in MTV's competitive success is its ability to understand its customers, as we have seen. The success of its consumer marketing strategy, which is focused and sustained, has enabled MTV to ride the waves even during economic downturns. For instance, Frank Brown, former president of MTV Networks Asia, Singapore, attributed MTV's success in Asia during the 1997/98 economic crisis in part to the following:

- Its focus on the youth market, which was not particularly hard-hit by the crisis. Youth viewed the crisis as a short-term blip in their lives, and spent accordingly.

- Its localization policy. "MTV provides a local programming mix to its Asian markets. Its high, glossy image, combined with local content, has given MTV a cult status and mass appeal."[4]

MTV leverages on its unique core competence to access young people, even to broadcast difficult behavior-change messages such as those to do with HIV/AIDS. The *Staying Alive* AIDS awareness program, which MTV co-produced with CNN and aired on November 27 and December 1, 2004, attracted more that a billion viewers worldwide. Hence, when world bodies such as the United Nations need to get a message to the youth of the world, they leverage on MTV's influence over young people. Bill Roedy, as chair of the Global Business Coalition, reiterated this point in 2001: "Half of the people newly infected with the virus were under 25 years of age: exactly MTV's audience. There was an enormous knowledge gap among that audience, which MTV could address, as well as the issue of stigma." MTV's image as the voice of youth is indubitable and remains the channel's key competitive success factor.

COMPETITIVE MAPPING

A company that is considered the market leader is usually exploiting some advantage over its competitors. Sustainable competitive advantage can only be effective through core competencies that are valuable, rare, and inimitable. In reality, sustainable competitive advantage is attainable through alertness, agility, and speed to react to any form of challenge. Conversely, first movers only have a temporary lead and are usually non-sustainable into a particular market without the strength of core competencies to fall back on.

MTV's number one positioning and sheer size, compounded by its accumulated brand equity and positive corporate reputation, render it an impenetrable fortress to most of its competitors. Most of the competition in the United States is insignificant. The only significant challenge in Europe was VIVA, a local German music channel that has since been guzzled up by MTV.

Asia is another story, with a real competitor—at least in terms of first mover advantage—in the form of Channel V, which has risen to challenge the MTV juggernaut. Channel V started in Asia well before MTV penetrated the region. However, over time, Channel V may not be able to withstand the full throttle of MTV's power. The competitive dynamics of MTV and Channel V are outlined below.

Competitive Strategy: MTV and Channel V

MTV's main competitive strategy, particularly in Asia, centers around localized programming; hence, the network's best response has been to make its local content as strong as possible. Also of note is its digital expansion toward providing mobile content.

MTV's closest competitor in Asia, Channel V, is owned by Rupert Murdoch's News Corp. Channel V was produced in and operated from Hong Kong from 1996 until 2002, when Double Vision took over its content production and moved operations to Malaysia. Channel V uses a "features and attributes" strategy to differentiate itself from MTV. The focus is on brand features and attributes that can be used to endorse the perception that Channel V is different from, or better than, MTV–or both.

To combat MTV's brand personality, which attracts a younger audience, Channel V is attempting to position itself as a more international and hip alternative in the Asian market. Channel V's efforts to revitalize its image are a response to, and an attempt to halt, MTV's aggressive expansion in Asia, especially since the mid-1990s. Thus, a comparative SWOT analysis of MTV and Channel V should give a clearer understanding of the subject.

Strengths

MTV's distribution covers all the major cities across Asia, affording advertisers an effective medium for targeting young adults (aged 15 to 34) in more than 150 million households across the region. MTV Chinese, MTV's Mandarin-language channel, reaches some five million households in Taiwan, about 265,000 households in Singapore, and more than 316,000 households in Hong Kong. MTV Southeast Asia reaches more than 20 million households in Indonesia, Malaysia, the Philippines, Singapore, Thailand, and Vietnam. MTV India reaches almost 20 million households in India, and MTV Korea reaches more than 1.6 million households in Korea.

An analysis of MTV's audience impact reveals that the network is Asia's most watched music channel, viewed by more young people aged 15–34 than any other music channel.

In terms of relevancy, up to 70% of MTV's playlist in Asia comprises local music videos, interspersed with international offerings. For example, MTV Chinese's playlist is 60% Mandarin and 40% international music, with several programs locally produced in Taiwan, such as *Mei Mei Watches MTV, Karaoke Box,* and *Gossip Corner.*

The network further augments this sense of belonging by fronting more than 30 local VJs from Taiwan, China, India, Indonesia, Malaysia, the Philippines, Singapore, Thailand, Vietnam, and South Korea to host local programs. MTV Southeast Asia offers customized programming hosted by local VJs speaking in Bahasa Indonesia, Bahasa Malaysia, Thai, Tagalog, and English. Such past local programs included *Seratus Persen Indonesia, Getar Cinta*, and *Salam Dangdut* (Indonesia); *MTV Diyes* and *Be Seen @ MTV* (Philippines); *MTV Syok, MTV Boom*, and *MTV Pulse* (Malaysia); *MTV Bangkok Jam* (Thailand); and *MTV Love Ballads* (Vietnam). The titles and nature of these programs change regularly to keep the brand fresh.

If the proof of the pudding is in the eating, then advertising and sponsorship is the main barometer of MTV's real power. MTV Networks Asia has more than 200 advertisers and some 40 program sponsors. These include some of the region's leading youth brands, such as Ericsson, P&G, Za, Sanyo, Coca-Cola, Nokia, Sony, Miller, EMI, Cadbury, Philips, Citizen, Reebok, Kahlua, Columbia TriStar, and 20th Century Fox.

In the music arena, the MTV-Billboard Asian Music Conference, first held in Hong Kong in 1998, has become a major forum in the music industry, bringing together movers and shakers from all over the world to discuss trends, challenges, and opportunities in the business. MTV's partnership with UNICEF and Levi's led to the Asia-wide "Speak Your Mind" campaign, which gives young people a voice on how to make the world a better place. Winners of the campaign were flown to New York to present an Asian Youth Charter to the then general secretary of the United Nations, Kofi Annan. MTV's roster of Youth Marketing Forums in various Asian countries has served as a showcase for case studies of effective youth marketing by leading regional and local consumer brands.

As part of its community outreach program, MTV has pioneered innovative social cause programs in Asia, such as the "Rock the Vote" campaigns in India, the Philippines, and Taiwan.

These programs serve as a platform for youth to express their views, and encourage young people to exercise their voting rights during national elections.

In comparison, Channel V takes the safe road; thus, its strength lies in playing familiar music. The image it portrays is that it knows everything there is to know about music, complemented with slick graphics; thus, its image is still very much that of visual radio. The fact that its parent company is Star TV gives Channel V a vast outreach in Asia, ranging from East Asia right across to the Middle East.

The keenest competition between MTV and Channel V is in India, where Channel V overtook MTV during the latter's short sojourn away from the subcontinent in the mid-1990s. However, MTV returned with a vengeance to claim back its territory and has been making decisive inroads into the Indian market ever since. Channel V's initial success has prompted a shift in MTV's programming mix. Hence, Channel V's personality remains largely international, daring, cheerful, and bold—although still very much visual radio, whereas MTV has forayed into the localization of music plus variety. Channel V's past glory as a first mover and its international high ground remain its strengths in India, yet it has followed its competitor's steps into lifestyle shows, thus acknowledging MTV's strength.

Between September 20 and October 18, 2003, Channel V claimed to have overtaken MTV as the number one music channel for the target audience aged 15–34 years in the six metro cities in India, according to data provided by TAM Media Research. This claim is disputed, however, because the data didn't encompass the whole country. The Conditional Access System (CAS) by which electronic transmission of digital media is limited only to subscribed clients, a system introduced by the Indian government to rein in the numerous cabsat (cable satellite) operators within the country, has also put a spoke in Channel V's wheel in India. In reality, Channel V trails MTV on the all-India platform. However, as the market share ratings for Asian cable media channels are still in their infancy, the results remain inconclusive and in doubt.

Weaknesses

In its rush to ride the localization train, MTV has encountered problems in compromising on its brand identity. For example, although localization was highly successful in India, it started going off tangent when MTV began to cash in on Indians' love for soap operas. While part of its organic growth, Indian soap operas were a far cry from MTV's offbeat signature shows such as *The Osbournes*. Too many subplots led the content off track from the network's music and youth focus, and would eventually have led to the dilution of MTV's brand identity. Frank Brown, former MTV Networks Asia Pacific president, said in 2005:

We know from our experience around the world that it is essential to stay true to your brand, to your music base, and to develop around the edges some content that has a different role to play—whether it is soap, movie, or fashion programming. You have to be careful on how far to go and how to do that in anything that actually takes a lot of your budget to develop... What we are not to do is to say that we are going to be a general entertainment channel, spend loads of money, and make these expensive shows only to find out later that the advertising revenue hasn't changed. You need to be careful and draw the balance as you put in creative ideas to press for organic growth.[5]

On the other hand, Channel V's perception problem as an MTV imitator isn't easy to shake off. This is to be expected with a competitor such as MTV and its number one global positioning stance. Channel V lacks the youthful *joie de vivre* of MTV as a result of a paucity of diverse programs.

Channel V's VJs are predominantly female, especially on the international channel. Although many of them are visually appealing, possessing hip, pan-Asian appearances, their personalities remain restrained. The VJs suffer from a positioning credibility, as they are largely disconnected from the masses. In recognition of this problem, Channel V is including well-known celebrities, such as Malaysian actress/singer Maya Karin as well as others from the Indian film industry, in its VJ line-up.

Although Channel V tries to differentiate itself as an all-music channel, its brand personality in most markets is conceived as conservative and serious, bordering on aggressive and arrogant, and appealing mainly to viewers over 25 years of age. This narrow audience base and market focus makes it difficult to gain the support of a younger audience. To counter this, Channel V created a program called *Remote Control*, which has been termed "fresh and fun," to cater specifically for a younger audience with what it calls a "string of hits, boy bands, requests and dedications, as well as on-air chats with the VJs and touring artists."

In India, particularly, Channel V has ventured into lifestyle programming à la MTV in order to interact with viewers. However, even advertisers acknowledge that MTV holds the advantage, as through sheer experience it has mastered the art of connecting, interacting, and having a dialogue with the audience. It is largely through advertising that one can gauge the success of each channel. MTV's 360-degree marketing approach, not to mention its one billion worldwide viewer base, provides the ultimate consumer connection that marketers yearn for. On top of that, VH1's recent entry into India has also been a threat to Channel V's international music leadership status, as well as to its older target audience. Hence, it is not an overstatement to say that MTV is the preferred choice of nearly all the top global and local brands.

Sunil Lulla, former general manager, MTV India, says:

> There is an increasing set of evolved marketers who—to address their market segment—need to talk, interact, and have a dialogue with the consumers. MTV is good at making a connection with the viewers, whether it's a campus-based show, a countdown show, a contest like the VJ hunt, or our promos. It could also be in the form of an off-air activity like the Club Dance in Bangalore. MTV has been bought by sponsors and advertisers because of the value it offers. This value comes through reach (seven million households), efficiency, the only youth-focused television medium, and a premium image (mutual brand allocation).

MTV will be difficult to combat due to its brand-building strategies, including special events such as the MTV Asia Awards, VJ hunts, and so on. In addition, MTV's 360-degree marketing has brought about tie-ups with local telecommunications provider DiGi in Malaysia, to provide a new youth service package to DiGi's customers. The package includes free unlimited MTV downloads, daily MTV gossip via text message, an exclusive WAP portal, an exciting Web portal, and special invites to parties, movies, concerts, and other "cool" events, among other attractive offers. It also allows users to expand their network of friends, share ideas and experiences, and utilize exciting services such as Friend Finder, Bubble Talk, and LifeLogger. "DiGi, being the first to launch a product tailored for youths, is exhilarated to announce its partnership with MTV, one of the most powerful and connected youth brands in the world," announced Chee Pok Jin, DiGi marketing officer, in 2005. Above all, the affordable pricing of the package makes it readily available to the mass market.

Channel V, on the other hand, has been perceived as riding on the coattails of its parent body, Star TV. Although it claims to attract its own advertising, Channel V's restructuring efforts, aimed at expanding its viewer base, speak volumes about the channel's actual hold over viewers in Asia.

Market Opportunities

The "MTV Nation" is literally a world without borders currently reaching one billion viewers worldwide. With the network's 100th channel, MTV Base, having been set up in Africa, young people all over the world—from New York, Rio de Janeiro, and Moscow, to Beijing, Jakarta, and Timbuktu—can now be a part of the "MTV Nation." "Now a large part of our future will be what happens outside the US, and that's exciting," said Tom Freston, former president and CEO of Viacom.

However, market expansion may not necessarily mean market penetration. Thus, it is important to consider market development and segmentation. In the United States, for example, MTV's Logo channel was introduced to cater for the gay market, in recognition of the increasingly diverse nature of American society.

In Asia, on the other hand, where there is slow penetration of cabsat television, MTV has turned instead to mobile telecommunications, which are highly popular and affordable in Asia, to deliver its content to viewers around the region.

The above suggests that MTV's market opportunities in the future could lie in the convergence of technologies. Anything that would have a strategic fit with MTV's vision—such as radio, print, production facilities, and digital media—would fall into this category. The network's collaboration to provide content for Microsoft's Xbox is another indicator of MTV's outlook for the future. Hence, the 360-degree marketing approach seems most appropriate for steering the MTV ship into the future.

Channel V began as a copy of MTV, a music channel complete with VJs; and like MTV, it is beginning to diversify its content via reality, adventure, and experimental programming. Although

Channel V claims to be an innovator—or maybe even a trailblazer—in terms of its content, it has found it difficult to shed the image of being an MTV imitator, because of the latter's number one positioning strategy.

Channel V tries to differentiate itself through its innovative content, such as *Pop Stars* (actually the Indian version of the *Idol* series), *Crush*, *P.O.V.*, and *BPL Oye!* in India. *Pop Stars* marked a watershed in expanding Channel V's viewership among the 15–34 age group. However, Channel V's success in the rest of Asia is less prevalent than in India, from which one could conclude that Channel V can only make its presence felt in MTV's absence. Although Channel V had an earlier presence in Southeast Asia, and shows such as *By Demand* are very much in the vein of MTV's *TRL* and *MTV's Most Wanted*, it has since been overshadowed by the later entrant to the market.

In an effort to expand its operations as well as market share, particularly in Southeast Asia, Channel V has partnered with Double Vision in Malaysia since 2002[6] to host its new production base in Kuala Lumpur for all its international programs broadcast throughout the region. Since then, Channel V and Double Vision have launched MTV-style hunts for fresh, local, on- and off-screen talent in an attempt to expand its viewer base through its localization strategy. Double Vision is making Channel V's presence felt within Malaysia and Singapore through its local network via national media coverage.

Former local VJs, including Maya Karin, an actress and singer of Malaysian–German parentage, and Sarah Tan, a Singaporean of Eurasian mix, have been incorporated as part of Channel V's attempt to localize, as well as to penetrate a younger market within the region. A couple of Channel V's VJs have already made a name for themselves within the region—namely, Asha Gill and Paula Malai Ali. At the time of writing, the most recent Channel V VJs are Alvin Puga a.k.a Alvey, Nicholas Saputra, Marion Caunter, Dominic Lau, and Joey G.

Market Threats

Although MTV seems almost invincible all over the world as a result of its localization policy and the convergence of technology, it may not be able to keep all pretenders at bay. Local music channels have sprung up all over the world and each keeps gnawing away at MTV's market share. The most obvious solution to date for MTV has been to swallow them up through acquisitions, as was the case with VIVA in Germany.

In Asian markets such as India, local music channels seem to be springing up like mushrooms after rain. India's vibrant cable and satellite market has given rise to many such local networks, apart from the main competitor, Channel V. One such entity whom MTV has considered acquiring is SS Music, which caters largely to the southern Indian market. The fact that such a channel is able to ruffle feathers at MTV indicates the level of threat local networks could pose in the lucrative Indian market.

In Southeast Asia, the national networks seem to pose the biggest challenge, as most of the authoritative establishments there are parochial in nature, albeit not as high-handed as in China. Although the authorities have stifled Southeast Asian society's creative juices for a considerable period, the current changes in the global arena have caused them to loosen their hold. Hence, we are seeing the rise of several MTV imitators; HITZ.TV on Astro in Malaysia, with a similar global–local blend, has begun to make waves in that country.

THE COMPETITIVE OUTLOOK

One can conclude that, apart from acquisitions, market threats can only be countered by MTV's 360-degree marketing approach as Asia's societies begin to mature and become sophisticated. Then again, time is on MTV's side.

In India, Channel V revamped its image by bringing in a younger set of VJs to appeal to a younger generation of viewers, while also developing a host of lifestyle programs in a bid to compete with MTV. However, its strategy of reaching out to a younger audience may cause it to lose its older viewer base.

The tie-up with Double Vision in Malaysia has yet to make an impact in Southeast Asia. Channel V may be leveraging on Double Vision's network to garner more local media coverage, thereby pushing MTV into the shadows in a region where cabsat TV is not yet widespread. For several years, local TV stations have been giving airplay to some of Channel V's programs, thus cornering a favorable location for expanding its viewer base. This pseudo-entry barrier created by Channel V to block MTV's media exposure is being broken down via the latter's 360-degree marketing efforts, as mentioned earlier.

The Verdict? MTV Wins

MTV's music, visuals, and style entertain and satisfy a myriad of viewers across the entire world. The network practically unites the youth of the world as the standard-bearer for global youth culture by informing its viewers about modern lifestyles. Viewers relish the two-way connectivity that allows them to interact with MTV, thereby creating a tangible relationship as well as enhancing the intangible emotional quotient.

Finally, but importantly, MTV is constantly keeping its momentum up by reinventing itself, thereby demonstrating that it truly understands its audiences' need for innovation. In view of all these advantages and more, it would not be out of place to suggest that no competitor could keep pace with MTV.

The issue now, from a brand perspective, is how will the brand continue to develop across all cultures and countries of the world? The answer lies in MTV's model of a brand development continuum.

THE BRAND DEVELOPMENT CONTINUUM

During its evolution, MTV has used a brand development continuum model (see Figure 7.1) to adjust how it manages the brand in

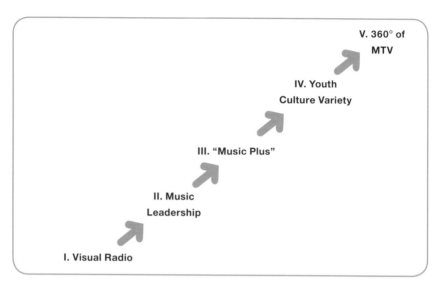

Figure 7.1 MTV Brand Development Continuum: The Variety of Ways They Connect with Us

countries and cultures that are in different stages of development, in order to connect with youth audiences.

MTV has evolved from its humble beginnings as visual radio to its current status as the standard-bearer for youth culture and variety. Music continues to be the foundation of the brand, despite the inception of lifestyle programs featuring youth culture. The creation of lifestyle programs that traveled more successfully than music was necessary, as the latter alone wasn't enough to fuel the growth of the brand. MTV's number one global viewer benefit is "seeing what's new" on the channel. Hence, the evolution from visual radio to youth culture and variety was inevitable.

"Personal relationships" is MTV's number one global viewer value, giving an insight as to why programs such as *Real World*, and *Room Raiders* rate highly with MTV's audiences. On the other hand, social issues become top of mind for viewers when the issues on hand are personally relevant. MTV Asia Aid 2005 was held concurrently with the MTV Asia Awards as a fundraising event for victims of the 2004 Asian Tsunami, but was also intended to show MTV's concern for its Asian viewers who were directly affected by the tragedy.

On the other hand, MTV's efforts to raise awareness of global poverty, mainly in Africa, resound more in the West because of the geopolitical and historical proximity between the two continents. HIV/AIDS is a common denominator worldwide, but MTV has taken it a step further through its innovative efforts to bring awareness to the youth of the world. This has proved fruitful in some conservative societies such as India, where MTV initiatives such as its "Staying Alive" campaign have rung alarm bells about the advent of the pandemic in the sub-continent and helped counter the denial found in the government and society at large.

More recently, in 2006, MTV combined efforts with "ONE, the Campaign to Make Poverty History" to fight global AIDS and extreme poverty. The "ONE Click Spot" was aired during the popular *TRL* program and featured music and movie stars such as Gwen Stefani, Jewel, Brad Pitt, George Clooney, Bono, and others. In the spot, each celebrity clicked his or her fingers to show that every three seconds a child dies of AIDS and extreme poverty, and that if millions of Americans come together as ONE, they can save an enormous number of lives. The MTV broadcasts built on the "Live 8" events, including the "Live 8" concerts.

Supporting spots rolled out across MTV, MTV2, mtvU, and MTV Overdrive, asking viewers to visit www.one.org. As Ian Rowe, vice president of strategic partnerships and public affairs at MTV, said: "MTV is honored to host the ONE SPOT across our platforms in our continuing efforts to bring awareness to global AIDS and poverty. It is possible to end poverty, so we hope it will be another tool to engage our audience on these dire issues and inspire them to be part of a fight."

Also in 2006, MTV commenced a partnership with The Body Shop. The campaign to raise funds for research into, and awareness of, HIV/AIDS is called "Spray to Change Attitude."

The MTV brand development continuum has taken its cue from the needs and wants of the target audience. An immense amount of market research focuses around the average teenager's point of view, regardless of where he or she may be from. Qualitative studies help to determine emerging trends, what is considered "cool," and which forces are shaping trends. The forces that drive the MTV brand ascertain that the channel exists as an honest reflection of youth culture. This fact is even more pertinent among the Millennials segment of youth, who are empowered by a combination of technological and economic booms as well as stronger parental bonds, diversity, and spiritual astuteness.

From Visual Radio to Music Leadership

The Millennials' penchant for personal expression is also a strong trend driver that has been a major part of the MTV brand evolution and creative process. The reason for this is that the Millennials literally grew up with a remote control in their hands, thereby giving them the power to control their own media. Hence, the reality that MTV learnt early on was that passive visual radio without any interaction wasn't enough to hold the attention span of this fickle generation. Shows such as *TRL*, designed to empower viewers to choose the videos they wanted to see, and *FANatic*, which enabled viewers to interview celebrities, were the result of these findings. Thus, the MTV brand evolved from visual radio, which had outlived its novelty, toward an empowered, interactive, viewer-centered media experience.

Music Plus Youth Culture Variety

MTV literally has immersed itself in the reality of its audiences' music, art, and lifestyles, accepting the evolution of youth culture as the reality of its brand continuum. In its quest to reflect the lifestyles of young people around the world, MTV has remained an honest voice as an expression of the purest form of art. It is in this area that MTV walks a fine line of fulfilling its social responsibilities without compromising its audiences' trust.

MTV practices non-censorship as part of its efforts to express art in a pure and honest manner, although it doesn't allow violence and certain language that goes beyond regular television network standards. MTV's coverage of Spring Break, where college kids let loose for a week, is an example of how the channel takes an honest approach to the subject of rites of passage in youth culture. MTV's programming division deliberates on research, as well as music videos, to decide which artists and programming ideas are most likely to create a "buzz" among its target markets. The deciding factor is to know what the audience likes, and the key success factors that will connect with the viewers. This is the essence of MTV's brand development continuum, which eventually turns trends and fads into a wider acceptance as youth culture.

Localization to tailor MTV's services to specific audience demographics and music tastes is another significant milestone in the continuum of the brand. For instance, MTV Brazil oozes sex appeal; MTV Italy is designed to appeal to style-conscious young Italians, with cooking and fashion shows featuring heavily in its programming mix; and a show such as *Spring Break* would never be aired in religiously conservative Indonesia.

From visual radio, to music leadership, to music plus youth culture variety, MTV's brand continuum has finally found its true identity, in its coexistence with the expression of art and its social responsibility for educating its viewers. For example, MTV has introduced social awareness documentaries such as the Peabody and Emmy Award-winning *Choose or Lose*. The latter started in 1992 as a pro-democracy campaign to encourage up to 20 million people to register to vote, and hosted a town hall forum for Bill Clinton. It has become an ongoing program with the aim of promoting political awareness and voter registration and mobilization.

To help stop violence, MTV also introduced the Emmy Award-winning "Fight For Your Rights" campaigns, which have helped empower young people to take a stand against violence and discrimination, as well as help them get information and take charge of their sexual health. Taking the lead from its audience, MTV continues to create pro-social programming that speaks to young people's beliefs and desires.

360-Degree Marketing

MTV's brand continuum is evolving even further through its 360-degree marketing approach, which is expanding across a range of technologies. MTV is now providing its content via mobile phones, and even through interactive gaming, such as with the tie-up with Microsoft's Xbox in 2005. This provides further penetration into MTV's existing markets, on top of making it easier to break into new markets and to stay in touch with the trends of the tech-savvy Millennials.

> MTV International announced a three-year, $75 million agreement with Motorola that leverages new media to create a state-of-the-art mobile music environment. The thinking behind it? Says the King of Content, "We want to drive our content to every place and every platform on the planet." That kind of ambition and creativity is what drives the industry, according to Sumner Redstone. It's also what the consumer demands—and satisfying consumer demand, he says, will determine the winners in the media and entertainment company industry.[7]

The "MTV Nation" is always interactive, and their world is a continuum of entertainment, information, and communication. Thus, the tie-ups with multinationals such as Motorola and Nokia, and local telcos such as DiGi in Malaysia, not only put MTV on the cutting edge of technology, but also draw it closer to its attention-span challenged viewers 24/7. Hence, the essence of MTV's brand continuum that makes it the global standard-bearer of youth culture is its inimitable branded content.

RESEARCH AND CASES FROM DIFFERENT COUNTRIES

The MTV brand continuum ranges from the original visual radio format, to music leadership, to music plus variety, and finally to youth culture variety, but the implementation and adaptation depends on the particular generation or geographical location in question. This is because each generation or geographical location produces change, thus requiring an enormous amount of research and creative edge to stay ahead. Digital feeds also allow MTV to create channels to suit the myriad of music genres, such as rock, rap, techno, and so on. Despite the continuum of the MTV brand, the core values of being irreverent and youthful are maintained worldwide to create consistency and allow for instant global recognition.

Asia is a case in point. MTV initially had a regional service known as MTV Asia, which aired an odd mix of Western, Indian, and Chinese music that rendered the channel awkward in the indigenous regions. (Chinese songs would pop up when Indian viewers tuned into the channel, and vice versa.) There was a clear and urgent need for each country to have its own localized version of MTV to reflect the taste and demands of viewers in different markets. MTV Asia's local content comprises up to 80% of its programming, making it more accessible to different audiences and, hence, catapulting ratings. MTV in India, China, Thailand, and Indonesia remains decidedly local in flavor, but Southeast Asia—that is, Singapore and Malaysia—retains an international mix.

Examples of how the continuum is applied in two very different countries—India and China—can be found in Chapter 10. The next chapter analyzes further how MTV uses various tools in the execution of its brand to make it truly global and local.

1   "The Ultimate Synergy: MTV Asia and Golden Bytes Interactive,"
    Asianet, December 26, 2005,
    http://news.xinhuanet.com/english/2005-12/26/content_3971738.htm.
2   "The 100 Top Brands 2006," *BusinessWeek,* http://bwnt.businessweek.com/
    brand/2006.
3   Interbrand Best Global Brands 2007 Report, http://www.ourfishbowl.com/
    images/fishbowlstory/2672007/bestglobalbrands_2007ranking.pdf.
4   World Economic Forum, "The Asian Consumer Market: Identifying Trends
    and Winning Strategies," East Asia Economic Summit, October 19, 1999,
    http://www2.weforum.org, http://www2.weforum.org/site/
    knowledgenavigator.nsf/Content/The%20Asian%20Consumer%20Market_
    %20Identifying%20Trends%20and%20Winning%20Strategies_19997cef.
    html?open.
5   Interview with Frank Brown, *www.Indiantelevision.com*, July 11, 2005,
    http://www.indiantelevision.com/interviews/y2k5/executive/
    frank_brown.htm.
6   *Wikipedia,* http://en.wikipedia.org/wiki/Channel_V.
7   "The King of Content: An interview with Summer M. Redstone, chairman
    and CEO Viacom," *Outlook Journal*, June 2004, http://www.accenture.com/
    Global/Research_and_Insights/Outlook/By_Alphabet/TheKingOfContent.htm.

8

Brand
Execution:
Giving Youth a Total
Music Experience

In the early chapters of the book we took an in-depth look at what youth wants and needs, and what they demand from an entertainment brand. This chapter focuses on the main means by which MTV satisfies these needs via its tactical brand initiatives.

CONTESTS

A passion for music is the root of the MTV brand. MTV recognizes the importance of music in its programming and content, and is able to use music to draw in fans of the artists. One way it does this is by giving fans access to their favorite artists. For example, when Kelly Clarkson, the first-ever "American Idol"-turned-popular pop singer, embarked on a world tour, MTV Asia ran a contest, the winners of which from Singapore, Malaysia, the Philippines, Thailand, and Indonesia got to fly to attend Clarkson's concert in Sydney. One lucky winner even got to be the singer's personal assistant for the day.

The following extracts from testimonies by winners of MTV contests indicate that the channel is able to fulfill MTV fans' need for extraordinary music experiences, along with their dreams of meeting their favorite artists.

> Thank you MTV for giving me this chance to explore the unknown and be happy! Keep supporting MTV and you'll get a chance of a lifetime to make your dreams come true!
>
> Angelina, Singapore, 2005

> Winning the chance to meet Marion Raven was one of the best things I ever had in my life... MTV gave the fans a chance for a private showcase and it was amazing.
>
> Jassica and Kiran, Singapore, 2005

> I met my dream rock band The Darkness at Hilton Bay (they were so cool!) and got our merchandise signed. All in all I have to say that MTV is where dreams become reality and it definitely was a once in a lifetime experience for me.
>
> Terence, Malaysia, 2005

MTV GOES BEYOND THE "CONVENTIONAL" MUSIC EXPERIENCE

Another creative way of giving fans access to their favorite artists is through filming documentaries about stars' lives. For instance, the 2005 *Jennifer Lopez: Beyond the Runway* show was an hour-long MTV special that gave viewers access to Jennifer Lopez's very hands-on approach to running her fashion company, while juggling her already demanding schedule.

This successful show has led to a new program called *Dancelife*. The show features Jennifer Lopez as the executive producer of a series about the real world of dancers working to make it in Hollywood. MTV.com says: "From soundstage to center stage, dance studio to dance floor, follow six dancers as they give their all to achieve their dreams in an intensely competitive profession where one good audition can launch a career and a bad attitude can finish one."[1] They also quote Lopez as saying, "It's a tough life, and I want to show that struggle... These dancers have dedicated their lives to this, and honestly, the glory is not always there... It's something they do only out of love."[2]

In a similar vein, Nick Lachey and Jessica Simpson had a program together called *Newlyweds*. MTV followed Lachey, former 98 Degrees band member, as he expressed his passion for music and started building a solo career. The footage showed him building a studio inside his home, hiring producers and writers, and signing on with Jive Records. Fans were able to watch the process of making an album. MTV also uses music to smartly package its shows. For instance, a remake of the classic *Wuthering Heights* gave the "MTV Generation" something of a musical in a movie format that featured Aimee Osbourne (daughter of Ozzy and Sharon Osbourne).

MTV IS DEVOTED TO YOUNG PEOPLE

Interspersed throughout MTV's reality/lifestyle shows are programs that deal with young people's aspirations, and interesting and offbeat life opportunities.

Fashion Gauge

One of the needs of MTV's target audience is to know what is trendy and in fashion, and what isn't fashionable. MTV Overdrive's *Street Style Fall 2005* interviewed trendy young people on the streets of New York, as well as style gurus, to identify the latest fashion trends. "Customized urban chic" was identified as the popular choice. "Don't buy the brand because of the brand, but because it says something about you," advised Coltrane Curtis, MTV fashion VJ. Most interviewees had put a personal stamp on their brand choices.

Above all, the fashion styles depicted personal musical tastes. For example, one interviewee said that she had chosen her sneakers because they were reminiscent of those worn by the 1990s' rap group Run DMC. Another person was sporting Marc Jacobs sunglasses, similar to those worn by hip-hop star Jay-Z at the 2005 MTV Video Music Awards. The awards event is a showcase of youth culture in itself, with a wide variety of styles and brands being absorbed almost instantly by young people all over the world. Singer and fashion icon Gwen Stefani seized upon the opportunity presented by the 2005 Awards to dress from head to toe in her personal apparel brand, Glam, which was due to be launched in New York the same week. The power of music is a force to be reckoned with when one realizes the extent to which the Millennial Generation aspires after this celebrity culture. Many think nothing of paying through the nose for top brands: "The appetite for designer labels and anything associated with celebrity has helped push luxury sales in the United States to $525 billion last year, up from $450 billion in 2003. By 2010, Americans are expected to spend $1 trillion on luxury goods."[3]

Socially Aware Programming

Besides fashion, MTV focuses on issues that are close to the hearts of young people. mtvU, a channel devoted to college students, runs regular documentaries that reflect young college students' lives, as well as addressing social issues through public service announcements and news featurettes. MTV knows that its target youth market is well informed, especially about global events and social issues. An example of a program that reflected a young person's life was *My Life (Translated): College Dreams,* in which news correspondent SuChin Pak delved into the life of Sonia, a first-generation Mexican-American, who was trying to balance her college ambitions with the cultural expectations of her family. Viewers logged on to the *think* MTV section of MTV.com to learn more about Sonia, to hear about SuChin Pak's experience of producing this very personal series, and to get important information aimed at helping young Latinos faced with unique educational challenges.

MTV also looks at broader social issues, such as how to safeguard the environment, in an innovative and fun manner that young people can relate to. The series *Trippin'* followed Hollywood actress Cameron Diaz and a group of her close personal friends—singer Justin Timberlake, actor Jimmy Fallon, and rapper Talib—as they traveled to places such as Tanzania, which were devoid of luxurious trappings, to report on environmental protection issues. The show also gave viewers tips on how to protect the environment and ways to volunteer to help such causes.

A similar program featured actress Angelina Jolie's efforts to draw attention to the extreme poverty of people living in Africa. *The Diary of Angelina Jolie and Dr. Jeffrey Sachs* in Africa, which screened on *think* MTV on September 15, 2005, touched the hearts and minds of many young people.

Thanks to Angelina Jolie's diary, I found out what I can do to help. I didn't know what I could do to change the world because everything seemed so far fetched. Knowing how big an impact we can make, actually wiping out extreme poverty by 2015, gave me hope. I want to do all I can to contribute to the effort. Thank you for the inspiration. *Ashley, 18, Proctor, MN*

"How To" Programs

Finally, MTV also focuses on "how to" lifestyle programs aimed at empowering youth. For example, MTV Southeast Asia created quick beauty tip featurettes to appeal to female viewers. MTV got Pantene on board as sponsor of the vignettes, which were aired five times daily, as well as appearing online. This allowed viewers to interact with others on the site, to give feedback, and to contribute their own tips to those generated on the show.

Time and time again, MTV has been able to create programs that meet its viewers' four basic needs: "Entertain Me," "Inform Me," "Interact with Me," and "Innovate for Me." As a result, young people are able to find their identity, express themselves, learn how to do various things, connect with others, and much more (see Chapter 5).

INNOVATION: CHANGING WITH THE TIMES AND THE FICKLENESS OF YOUTH

In Chapter 4, we discussed the fickleness of youth and how the adage "here today, gone tomorrow" expresses the way young people today live their lives. MTV is catering to a generation that requires constant innovation.

MTV Networks India's Vikram Raizada, now no longer with the company, believed that MTV Networks always stood for the shape of things to come, whether it was "innovative programming, unique marketing properties, unexpected merchandising and now ... mobile interactivity." MTV is able to stay innovative by bouncing creative ideas around its extensive global network. For instance, to create an innovative advertising spot, an initial idea is passed around, with each recipient adding perhaps five seconds of content before passing it on to the next person. Ideas and input are freely exchanged. MTV refers to this exercise as the "exquisite corpse." This playful creativity between different channels around the world is a way of keeping the creative relationship fresh between each of the markets.

Sometimes, a great idea or a good show is creatively repackaged to retain its freshness. *Jackass*, a crazy stunt show that pushes the boundaries, was repackaged in Southeast Asia as *MTV Whatever Things*. The stunts were toned down to suit the more tepid, moderate attitudes of Asian youth. Also, the reality series *Real World* is filmed and showcased in different cities, depicting their different lifestyles, habits, and plot lines. Being on top of social trends helps MTV in being innovative with its programming. For instance, changing child-parent relationships in the United States were the impetus for MTV to create *The Osbournes* show, to more accurately depict family life today.

One way to remain innovative is to create key "light switch" moments, which are linked to viewing highs. Viewer high times are associated with seasonal events (such as the start of the summer holidays, or when school resumes) or with post-event activities after shows such as MTV Video Music Awards. MTV leverages on the seasons in order to stay innovative, and to introduce new twists to programs such as *TRL*, for high school kids in the afternoon when school is out, and *Summer on the Strip*, as part of taking MTV's shows on the road to create more excitement for viewers.

CONNECTION: PERSONAL TOUCH POINTS/INTERACTIVITY

The value of music videos as a means of connecting and interacting with viewers has a lot to do with the power and influence of music in a young person's life. The visualization of music brings the viewer close to the artist, allowing them to see the artist's emotions and directly receive his or her message. Pioneering artists of the music video phenomenon, such as Michael Jackson, experienced record sales of their albums. Tapping into this communicative aspect of music videos, MTV began creating music video shows that revolve around the viewer.

MTV has moved beyond just music videos to creative live and reality shows, such as *TRL*, in order to provide that connection and interactivity. Just playing music videos, a common staple of MTV, was revamped to create more excitement. The success of the show hinges on the fact that viewers can vote for their favorite videos to be featured. This heightens the viewer's sense of participation and personal connection. *TRL* also gives viewers the option of taking a behind-the-scenes tour of the show, playing with live webcams, and the chance of being made "Fan of the Week." This interactive strategy transports viewers directly from their homes to the countdown action at New York City's Times Square.

MTV Southeast Asia's *Most Wanted* is in a somewhat similar vein, with viewers sending in requests for their favorite music videos to be aired on the program. The videos with the most number of requests receive air-play, which gives viewers an update on the most popular music making waves in the region.

In 2005, MTV took further steps to make interactivity a common element of its music shows. For example, MTV Southeast Asia has *Chart Attack, Pop Inc*, and *Pick and Play,* all of which feature participation by viewers either on air, or by text message. This interactivity/connection feature has also spread to MTV India, which launched an interactive show in mid-2005 to give viewers the opportunity to communicate with the channel in real time via text message. (See the case study on MTV India in Chapter 10.) Considerable time and money have been spent on making the MTV brand as interactive as possible, although it was approachable even in the early years through conventional means of communication, such as by mail, phone, and fax, before email and text messaging became popular.

MTV isn't concerned just with building a relationship with the audience, but with getting them to respond to MTV. Getting viewers to participate in roadshows, casting calls, selective internships, and social causes organized by MTV are just a few ways in which the channel connects with its target audience.

MTV also has a very broad perspective because it spends a lot of time analyzing research from research houses, and employing trend spotters, teen consultants, and anthropologists. MTV constantly engages its target audience in focus groups, both to test and understand ideas.

INTEGRATED MARKETING COMMUNICATIONS

Website Strategy

Professor Don Schultz of Medill School of Journalism at Northwestern University, in the United States, was one of the early pioneers of the principles of integrated marketing communications (IMC). He wrote: "Technology is what makes IMC possible, and the more rapidly technology diffuses, the faster IMC grows and matures. Because technology drives and supports IMC, it is not just another passing marketing fad or hot communications topic that will fade and die. Instead IMC is likely the future of all marketing communications.[4]

MTV has done exactly that in order to stay on top. It remains at the forefront of the minds of young people, through a 24/7, 360-degree approach, using technology to communicate the brand effectively and to meet its target audience at all consumer touchpoints. One of the first mediums employed to fulfill MTV's 360-degree strategy was the World Wide Web. MTV.com, which began in 1996, made MTV available 24/7 to its target audience. This fits the profile of its audience, since MTV viewers also lead a 360-degree lifestyle, saturated with technological gadgets such as televisions, computers, stereos, and mobile phones.

MTV.com was developed not just as a promotional/marketing extension, but as a programming destination where qualities such as community, interactivity, and broad, deep music access are an essential part of the website. Every page on the website reflects the 360-degree philosophy. For instance, users can gain access to their favorite artists' tour information, the latest music videos, and exclusive concert webcasts.

The websites are used as part of MTV's community-building efforts. Fans can build a membership profile, sign up to get exclusive newsletters, and use the message boards to communicate with friends. Viewers can also gain access to information about and footage of the personal lives of their favorite artists. If the message boards aren't fast enough or sufficiently interactive, there is the MTV instant messenger option.

Finally, MTV.com also contains MTV Radio, where listeners can tune into 46 stations from a variety of genres as well as MTV-branded radio channels such as TRL [Total Request Live] and MTV2. This initiative establishes MTV Radio as a leading Internet radio station that offers streaming, and downloadable music with the option to purchase then and there.

Events: Youth Forums, Annual Shows, and Roadshows

MTV is the accepted authority on global youth, not only because of its presence in 164 countries around the world, but because it is known to understand youth, and is the cutting edge in terms of setting the trends. The PBS documentary *Merchants of Cool* put it this way: what MTV spots as a potential trend, is produced on their music videos which then translates to an accepted youth trend, because viewers who watch what their artists wear on their music videos will want to emulate them. Therefore, MTV is on the winning side: advertisers scramble for spots on its channels, and participate in MTV's global, annual youth forums that enlighten and educate companies who are targeting the same market as MTV.

MTV communicates its brand through events that it sponsors, and it builds up hype about its brand through its annual music award shows. Other shows such as the *VJ Hunt* in Asian countries such as Thailand, Malaysia, India, and the Philippines are hyped up through pre-event publicity bashes, with hordes of young people showing up at the audition venues to interact with current MTV VJs and try their hand at skits, stage presentations, and short on-camera stints. MTV continues to hype the process by staging final showdowns at popular clubs in Kuala Lumpur, followed by parties hosted by MTV's VJs. Fans are pampered at these events, and loyalty breeds as they cheer on performances by famous artists, participate in fun games, and win "cool" prizes and door gifts.

Another outdoor event that MTV leverages to reach its target audience is *Nokia Unwired at Hard Rock Live*. The event was held in Florida, in the United States. Artists such as the Ying Yang Twins, My Chemical Romance, Weezer, Mike Jones, and Good Charlotte performed before a live audience on location. These innovative musical events not only celebrate today's musical experience, but also give MTV's viewers the opportunity to discover what is new within the music industry.

MTV also employs inconspicuous marketing tactics in unexpected environments to promote its brand. For instance, *Boiling Point* is a reality comedy show in which pranks are played on passers-by. MTV's crew is dropped off in a crowded mall, a restaurant, or at a beach, where they make an embarrassing scene and cause a racket, with the purpose of seeing how long people will tolerate the disturbance. The reactions of the onlookers can vary from amusement, to disgust, to real anger. When it is revealed that it was actually a stunt by MTV, the crowd usually accepts with good grace that it has been the butt of the joke. MTV Asia's localized version of the show—*Boiling Point—Malaysia Edition*—was a similar success.

Mobile Phone Strategy

Part of MTV's strategy for being in touch with its consumers 24/7 is to offer its content via mobile phone. In 2003, MTV International signed a three-year, US$75 million agreement with telecommunications giant Motorola to create a state-of-the-art mobile music environment for MTV's viewers. The groundbreaking joint venture, which is part of the network's 360-degree marketing approach, puts MTV far ahead of the competition as it continues to be focused on satisfying consumer demands. "We want to drive our content to every place and every platform on the planet," said Sumner M. Redstone, chairman and CEO, Viacom, in June 2004.

> For Redstone, branded content is the name of the game, and MTV, the global youth culture channel, is the "mother lode of Viacom brands." His faith in MTV is virtually limitless—and hard to fault. That kind of ambition and creativity is what drives the industry, according to Redstone. It's also what the consumer demands—and satisfying consumer demand, he says, will determine the winners in the media and entertainment company industry.[5]

MTV is also in partnership with other mobile phone companies in other countries, such as DiGi in Malaysia, offering downloads and mobile content such as ringtones, wallpapers, updated information, and privileged access to concerts and events sponsored by MTV for as low as US$1.50. Further to that, MTV is moving toward crafting content for mobile video phones: the 3Gs and 4Gs of this world (see Chapter 11).

VJ Strategy

An important aspect of MTV's VJ requirements is that the person must be compelling on air and able to connect and engage with the audience. Thus, MTV's VJs need to embody MTV's brand personality as well as their own individual personalities. The qualities of MTV— being *relevant, passionate, unpredictable, clever, really funny, risk-taking, bold, open, and no bullshit*—are manifested in terms of local culture, current global and local trends and fads, as well as viewers' lifestyles, opinions, and values. Hence, the VJ strategy is to have those who are as close to the target market as possible, in order to reflect relevant views and speak to the audience in a manner that viewers can relate to.

The role of MTV's VJs

MTV's VJ Carson Daly, the ever-approachable host of *TRL*, is a case in point. Daly's accessible, personable, metrosexual style was

a strong drawcard for viewers, who felt they could relate to him.

SuChin Pak, MTV's news correspondent, is the ambassador for the channel's embracement of diversity. Viewers find her confident, stylish, charming, yet happy-go-lucky manner very refreshing. They feel they can relate to her, while also relying on her to be informative and professional. Pak applies an anthropological eye when it comes to connecting with the audience.

In a different vein, VJ Cyrus Broacha is MTV India's secret weapon. Even his competitors concede difficulty in combating his popular appeal and whacky, out-of-the-box thinking. The popularity of MTV Southeast Asia VJs Denise and Utt is unparalleled, to the extent that competitors have begun to churn out copies of the pair.

The VJs add to the freshness of the MTV brand and keep alive its appeal by interpreting the brand personality in their own ways. This appeal and freshness are paramount to MTV's competitive strategy.

MTV's VJs have grown beyond being just program presenters, to become knowledgeable music journalists in their own right, competent at interviewing celebrities and hosting their own television shows on MTV. The right VJ portrays the channel's image and personality. As MTV itself is ever evolving and reinventing itself, the VJs also are encouraged to be themselves and to explore new dimensions. This adds to the appeal of the channel. Hence, knowledge of music isn't the only criterion for a successful MTV VJ; an attractive screen presence and the ability to project a "cool" image on screen are equally as important.

MTV's VJs also represent a vast selection of musical genres appealing to a smorgasbord of cultural ethnicities. For example, in India the VJs speak Hinglish, a mix of English and Hindi, to complement the Bollywood cultural elements that MTV India has incorporated into its brand strategy.

VJ Utt: Epitome of Metrosexuality.

Appearances play a large part in Asian culture, even among young males who have embraced

> The channel (MTV India) embraced Bollywood and launched a nationwide hunt for new veejays. (One winner was a former Miss India.) ... notably *MTV Bakra*—the word means "goat" in Hindi—an Indian-style *Candid Camera* in which the host, Cyrus Broacha, plays gags on unsuspecting people... Broacha, who has both a goofy and a sober persona, has become the most famous face of MTV India; he interviewed Bill Gates when the Microsoft chairman wanted to speak to India's young people about AIDS. Says media buyer Divya Gupta: "Their content is now completely tailored to Indian youth."[6]

the "metrosexual" trend with gusto. The current fascination with the pan-Asian look in Asia is compounded by the trend to dye one's hair color lighter than the uniformity of black Asian hair, and by the soaring sales of skin whitening products, as opposed to tanning products in the West. Hence, it comes as no surprise that MTV Southeast Asia's pan-Asian VJ Utt (Thai national Greg Uttsada Panichkul) is the current "dream guy" of many young Asian girls. His "metrosexual" image of tinted blond hair, green eyes, and scrubbed features, along with his infectious personality and his ability to speak impeccable American-accented English as well as Thai, sits well with young Asians. Utt's trendy persona gels with the aspirations of young Asians, and as the VJ of the interactive show *MTV's Most Wanted*, he connects with his audience in a personal way through his friendly and entertaining manner. "*MTV's Most Wanted* is cool 'coz you have requests coming in from the kids, so it's actually their show," Utt commented in 2002.

VJ Denise: Lethal Combination of Smarts and Sexiness.

VJ Denise Keller of MTV Southeast Asia is the epitome of stimulating and aspirational, being a "lethal combination of smartness and sexiness," according to *FHM* magazine. Winner of the Ford Supermodel of the World, Singapore, in 2000, Denise is of mixed German and Chinese parentage. Her stunning looks, and innovative and stimulating personality, are enhanced by her intellect, aspirations, and sense of humor. Despite the glamorous, outer veneer, the model and host of *MTV's Most Wanted*, and numerous other productions, remains true to herself as part of the Millennial Generation, even to the point of being an animal lover who adds to her weirdness quotient by including an internship with a snake charmer! She told *FHM* magazine in 2003:

> As a VJ, you have to balance looking good, presenting good and always being on top of things... People think I'm a VJ and it's all fun and games. But my passion is getting to know people and learning from them. A lot of it has to do with spirituality and what is inside them rather than what is the outside.[7]

VJ Hunts. Finally, how does MTV find the right people to be its public face? One way is by conducting VJ hunts. MTV sees the VJ hunt as an opportunity to connect with young people, which is essentially MTV's business mission. Starting with the invitation for applicants, through to the auditions and selection of suitable candidates, the buzz factor created is enough to make young people feel the relevancy and personal touch of MTV. The time, research, and effort needed to source relatable and informed VJs strengthens MTV's number one positioning strategy in an imitable fashion.

MTV's *VJ Hunt* in itself is an event to be reckoned with. The first such hunt was conducted in India in 1998; the practice has now spread to other MTV stations in Asia, with the most recent event being held in Indonesia in May 2007. From MTV's perspective, selecting the right VJs takes the channel forward, because the VJs are a part of the brand's personality. Therefore, VJ hunts are the perfect strategy for introducing new blood and new life into the channel, and for continually reinventing MTV's scope of appeal. As part of the VJs' jobs, they are encouraged to do their own thing, and to try new things to add to the MTV flavor.

VJ hunts also prove to be profitable for the channel, as they attract advertising dollars. For example, in 2005, MTV Southeast Asia had DiGi in Malaysia as a co-sponsor of the show. It is money well spent, given the popularity of the show with those advertisers targeting the youth market.

VJ hunts appeal to young people because they give them an opportunity to fulfill their aspirations. Young people have dreams and fantasies about appearing on television, being in show business, and being hailed as the next "hottest" thing. For a 2002 VJ hunt in India, MTV advertised for applicants as follows: "Ever fantasize about a career that can offer you fame, glamour, miles of travel to exotic locales, face-to-face chats with the best in Bollywood and around the world and yet pays you loads of money?" Even those young people not aiming to become a VJ can still participate via online/text message voting.

The talent hunt attracts people from all walks of life, from engineering students to teachers who are ready to give up their careers for a stint of fame. What exactly does MTV look for? MTV India says it looks for someone who loves music, speaks well, and is able to add something unique to the channel. Anyone who seems "with it" or "in," and with a sense of music and diction, and the right looks and attitude, stands to grab the coveted role.

The show normally has a 16-episode structure to showcase the makeover process.

Distribution

In the age of consolidation, cable network operators are banking on synergy, sharing of resources, utilizing multiple platforms, and partnering with corporations such as Microsoft. On October 14,

2005, MTV announced its partnership with Microsoft, which was aimed at expanding MTV's reach of its broadband channels into every room in the house through Microsoft's Windows XP Media Center Edition 2005 PCs. With that and an Xbox 360 game console, users will have the ability to switch seamlessly between a standard TV experience and on-demand broadband programming without having to leave the couch. Broadband channels such as MTV Overdrive will debut on the software. Through this partnership, MTV is providing its target audience with the ability to connect with MTV's content on every platform, by distributing the channel in various forms and helping viewers to take their entertainment experience to the next level.

MTV Overdrive was launched in the United States in 2005. It is now available to users all around the world who have broadband Internet access. MTV Overdrive is the industry's leading broadband content provider, with 47 million streams of music videos, MTV News, and companion programming content. Specifically, MTV Overdrive delivered 13 million unique streams of its "My VMA" content during its 30 day-run, giving fans the opportunity to re-experience exclusive performances from the 2005 MTV Video Music Awards, stream interviews with artists, and check out the VMA fashions from the white carpet. MTV Overdrive also premiered the next generation of MTV's famous performance series, *Unplugged*, featuring the incomparable Alicia Keys. In just one week in September 2005, MTV Overdrive recorded over a million streams of the *Unplugged* performance, making it the most popular programming on the broadband network for that time period. MTV Overdrive is still an ongoing and successful program.

With the advent of 3G wireless mobile phones, as well as 2G phones, companies such as Motorola, in partnership with MTV, get to provide mobile content such as mobisodes (a mobile episode). For the first time, MTV and Motorola are creating a series of eight short mobisodes for a program called *Head and Body*, which follow the comedic adventures of a character whose head is detached from his body. Beginning October 20, 2005, mobisodes were disseminated through MTVNI's mobile distribution channels via Motorola's website, www.hellomoto.com, in markets across the Asia Pacific, Latin America, and Europe. The creation of this first-of-its-kind series has enabled MTV to pioneer unique ways of storytelling, and of connecting with young people as they turn to this new platform of entertainment, their handsets. It is the "third screen," a new distribution channel separate from cable TV and broadband channels.

Since 2001, MTV has seized the opportunity to use the wireless platform to make its Video Music Awards available to mobile users. With the growing popularity of cell phones, personal digital assistants, and other handheld devices, MTV realized that an effective medium for strengthening brand awareness would be to provide mobile content to companies such as DiGi, in Malaysia. Together with DIGI, marketing promotions, perks, and content are distributed to mobile users. The DiGi MTV Powerpack also offers free access to parties at "cool" clubs in Kuala Lumpur. MTV Mobile steers consumers to the Internet, where they can download MTV logos to put on their mobile phones and ringtones that sound like a variety of international artists.

In terms of a conventional cable satellite distribution channel, MTV continues to partner with platforms such as One Alliance in India. Digital television entertainment such as DIRECTV is another of MTV's distribution channels, especially for the latest programs explains:

In the Philippines, *MTV in Print*, a magazine with a circulation of about 25,000, helps to drive the brand. MTV is focusing on increasing the readership of the magazine, rather than subscriptions, which indicates that it wants to use as many distribution channels as possible, in order to get the brand out there. What young people can't get on TV, they can get on *MTV in Print*.

It is clear from this chapter that MTV has to translate its brand into action in a multitude of ways, yet in a consistent manner. The following chapter follows this theme and looks at how the MTV brand has been managed. It is one thing to have strategies in place, but an altogether different thing to manage them. As you will see, brand management is a complex process.

[1] Synopsis of *Dancelife*, *www.mtv.com*, http://www.mtv.com/ontv/dyn/dancelife/series.jhtml.

[2] Ibid.

[3] Mark de la Vina, "'Gold-collar' workers chase luxury on blue-collar salaries," *San Jose Mercury News*, July 27, 2005, http://www.azcentral.com/arizonarepublic/arizonaliving/articles/0727goldcollar.html.

[4] Don E. Schultz, *Marketing News*, February 15, 1993.

[5] "The King of Content: An interview with Sumner M. Redstone, chairman and CEO Viacom," *Outlook Journal*, June 2004, http://www.accenture.com/Global/Research_and_Insights/Outlook/By_Alphabet/TheKingOfContent.htm.

[6] Marc Gunther, "MTV's Passage to India." *Fortune,* August 9, 2004, http://money.cnn.com/magazines/fortune/fortune_archive/2004/08/09/377904/index.htm.

[7] *FHM*, 2003.

9

Brand Management

INTRODUCTION

Brand management is a process that tries to control everything a brand says and does, in order to keep the integrity of the brand vision, personality, and positioning. It's a tough job, as it demands that managers and guardians of the brand keep their eyes on the "big picture" while managing meticulously the day-to-day activities and exposure of the brand. The tough nature of brand management is compounded by the fact that another of its aims is to retain consistency, and to balance this with the need for change.

People who like and buy into a brand want the security of knowing that it won't change its character. Just as we are uncomfortable with people who suddenly and unpredictably change their mood and character, perhaps viewing them as somewhat schizophrenic, as consumers we want the security of knowing that our favorite brands will always be as we have known them. However, we also want the brand to change with us as our needs and lifestyles change; in other words, it needs to remain relevant to our lives. Therein lies the brand management dilemma of how to balance consistency with change.

With a global brand, there are tremendous challenges in managing this dilemma, as consumer demands across markets vary, and total exposure creates millions of moments of truth each day in terms of how the brand performs consistently but with relevance. This is especially difficult for a media brand such as MTV, which has almost non-stop exposure every day of every year.

Normally, global brand management is highly systemized, with committees, councils, equity boards, and the like. The amazing thing about MTV is that, not only does it manage its brand very successfully, but it does so without seeming to have a standardized brand management process or a dedicated organizational structure for doing so.

With these points in mind, this chapter will address several issues concerning the management of the MTV brand, namely:

- How does it keep the demographic range happy, when the needs of segments within it are very different?
- How does it balance consistency with change?
- How does it manage its heritage with different cultures?
- How does it use the brand personality to best effect?
- How does it keep its "product" fresh and relevant?
- How much autonomy is given to local programming?
- Does it have a brand management system?
- How is the MTV brand culture developed?

The answers to these questions are contained in the following descriptions of MTV's unique offerings. It is important to note that the key to MTV's success in dealing with these issues lies in its brand management skill—in particular, how it

- understands its customers;
- uses speed, flexibility, and innovation to the full; and
- sticks close to its values at all times.

MTV doesn't get it right all the time—no brand does—but mostly it takes the right decisions at the right time. Perhaps an interesting start in looking at these challenges is to examine what might be viewed as a less successful attempt by MTV to understand its customers and provide them with what they want.

GAINING NEW VIEWERS AND KEEPING THE AGING FAITHFUL

MTV's target audience is officially within the ages of 18 and 34; however, it is a known fact that younger people do view it regularly, so in reality it covers an age span from 15 to 34. This poses some challenges. First, MTV cannot rely on long-term brand loyalty, since the audience always ages and moves on. Second, as MTV enters its third decade, it is in a constant battle to gain new viewers and to maintain relevance in a modern popular culture. Third, it has to contend with the challenges posed by different geographic regions. MTV has attempted to deal with these issues in a variety of ways.

MTV World

MTV World was an example of how MTV tried to gain new viewers from the growing population of young, acculturated Asian-Americans. Under this umbrella brand title of MTV World, MTV Desi first went to air in the United States in July 2005. It was followed by MTV Chi, for Chinese-Americans, at the end of 2005; and by MTV K, for Korean-Americans, in 2006. These channels were modeled on their target audiences—hybrids, blending here and there, and grappling with identity issues, mostly in English. The rationale for such programs, gleaned from research, was that these second-generation immigrants not only desired their own age-appropriate connection to their parents' homeland, but were also passionate about seeing their struggle to define themselves as hyphenated Americans mirrored on television.

MTV Desi served as the prototype. It was a mixture of Bollywood videos, electronic tabla music and English-Gujarati hip-hop, and documentary clips profiling current "desis" (people or things of South Asian origin). The program included comic skits about South Asian-American generational conflicts, interviews with bicultural artists who act as role models by managing to balance the two cultures they reflect, and live shows of desi house parties.

MTV Chi played a mix of Mandarin rock, Mandopop, Cantopop, and Chinese-American rap and hip-hop. Music videos imported from Taiwan, Hong Kong, and China, as well as original programming, showcased up-and-coming artists from the United States and around the world.

It is clear that these spin-off networks were an attempt by MTV to capture nominal viewers and turn them into loyal fans/ viewers by customizing content to their tastes. This was part of MTV's brand management strategy of "thinking local" and serving a niche market. Young Asian-Americans are hungry to see people like themselves on television. Mike Sherman, general manager of radio station KTSF, explained: "There was nobody on TV that was like them, except stiff stereotypical characters, nerds and martial artists. They never saw people who looked like or acted like themselves or their friends, portraying regular people—flaws, idiosyncrasies, and all."[1]

MTV World was part of MTV's strategy to be "glocal," even in the United States where the youth culture isn't a homogenized one. MTV's view appeared to be that young people, wherever they are, will watch international acts for only so long before they will want to see something of their own culture and their own backyard.

Nevertheless, this way of reaching different demographic groups didn't live up to expectations and MTV is still trying to get its strategy right in this respect. All three programs were taken off the air at the end of April 2007, and MTV World no longer operates. Presumably the programs didn't create offerings that the audiences felt positively strongly about, or the viewer figures were not substantial enough.

CONSISTENCY VERSUS CHANGE

There is one challenge that all brands have to face, and that is to produce constant change and evolution in products and yet retain consistency in brand values and the customer proposition. The music and entertainment industries are no different, and it is a fact that no network can stay the same for too long before it begins to lose its viewers. The challenge for MTV has always been greater than that experienced by network news channels such as CNN or Fox, because it targets a youthful demographic that will eventually grow older. This means that the longer the network stays in business, the more it needs to reinvent itself in order to attract new youth customers. And yet it must still stay in touch with its roots in order to retain old faithfuls for as long as possible.

Some of MTV's changes, such as the addition of reality shows to the content and the reduced emphasis on music videos in recent years, appear to be alienating previously faithful viewers. It could be argued that MTV is now known more for shows such as *Spring Break* and *MTV Video Music Awards*, or for reality shows such as *Road Rules, Undressed*, and *Room Raiders*, than for the traditional offerings of music videos. Cost may be a factor in favoring reality shows over music videos, although it is unlikely to have been the main driver of change. The fact remains that MTV has started to expand beyond just music video content because this is what it feels the audience wants. An example of planned evolution is given below for MTV2.

STICKING TO THE BRAND PERSONALITY

Striking a balance between consistency and change is further complicated by the need to retain a brand's personality. MTV's brand personality is *relevant, passionate, unpredictable, clever, really funny, risk-taking, bold, open, and no B.S.* As with most great brands, the personality is a set of characteristics or traits that are used to express the brand through employee behavior and brand communications.

A company or product can have only one true, strong personality. This basic personality can be tweaked, adjusted, and flexed to emphasize particular strengths or values that attract different customer groups, as long as it isn't stretched so far as to be unrecognizable. Nevertheless, different personality characteristics can be emphasized or brought out more strongly at different times, again like people.

The amount of "stretch" available to any brand is based upon knowledge of various market segments, and whether or not the personality characteristics will be suitable for communicating to them. Extensions to brands (or sub-brands) are always achievable, but there are limits to this possibility. The main criterion for success is still to retain what the brand stands for.

EXTENSIONS TO THE BRAND

Another, more successful way of reaching out to different market segments has been the creation of extensions to the MTV brand; channels that have different offerings for different groups of people. Typical of these extensions are MTV2, VH1, and mtvU. As we will see, MTV seems to be able to project its brand personality and retain its soul in these channels.

MTV2

MTV2's initial purpose, once the original MTV channel had started concentrating on reality television and soap operas, was to give music fans a place to see constant, commercial-free music videos.

Launched in August 1996, MTV2 (known as just "M2" until early 1999) was created to show alternative types of music and older music videos than shown on normal MTV programs, along with some current and mainstream content. For the first couple of years, before digital and satellite television became common place, MTV2 had very limited availability, and basically relied on college campuses that provided their students with satellite television. The channel broadcast live over the Internet; however, it was again a little too progressive, as few people at that time had broadband Internet connections.

A new lease of life was given to MTV2 in late 2000 when Viacom—MTV and MTV2's parent company—bought out the independent and popular "jukebox" music video channel known as "The Box." From January 1, 2001, The Box was substituted by MTV2, and this allowed the channel into millions of additional households.

As part of this development, MTV2 allowed commercials to be shown and programmed the types of videos it played by genre. Hip-hop and soul music was played for an hour every weekday, rock music every weekday at 9 a.m. and 9 p.m., and a new program, *MTV2 Request*, was also shown every weekday. *MTV2 Request* played only videos selected by online viewer requests. Another new show, *Control Freak*, started in 2001, also on weekdays; while one video was playing, viewers voted in real-time to select the next video from three choices to be played. The majority of the daytime schedule still featured a diverse mixture of music videos from the past and present.

MTV2 Evolves

For the first few years (1996–2001), MTV2's music videos ran on eight-hour repeats, so that the same videos repeated three times during a 24-hour period. A new set of videos would then start again the next day. The channel had only two VJs, who were rarely seen on-screen but selected all the music videos shown each day. After this initial period, MTV2 started to experiment with new programming.

In the spring of 2002, MTV2 altered its format. New shows included *Chart2Chart*, which aired the most popular videos from all the genre charts. *Spankin' New* showed the newest videos of the week; and *Extreme Rock* showcased hard rock and metal music by artists such as Iron Maiden and Guns N' Roses. *Riffs & Rhymes* featured bands that combined the sounds of rock and rap music, such as Linkin Park and Limp Bizkit, but the show lasted only until the summer of 2002, while *Extreme Rock*, *Spankin' New*, and *Chart2Chart* survived until 2003. Other shows also arrived as MTV experimented with a wave of evolutionary ideas.

During 2002–03, MTV2 phased out the format of just showing music videos every day. It adopted a new slogan, "*Where the music's at*," and featured other music-related shows such as *MTV Icon* specials, news documentaries, and countdowns. More and more changes took place as time went by. One significant example of innovation came during the 2002 Fourth of July weekend. Over this period, MTV2 featured *Box Set Weekend*, showing selected artists from past shows called *Artist Collection*, plus other MTV programs such as *Making the Video* and *Ultrasound*, and live performances where possible. *Box Set Weekend* contained the highest concentration of non-video programming to date on MTV2, and this began a trend for MTV2 to play fewer music videos and more old MTV specials. The risk here was the possible alienation of MTV2's original viewers, who were looking for music videos and not documentaries and interviews already available on MTV and VH1. But MTV2 claimed that its ratings increased as a result of incorporating documentaries, interviews, and behind-the-scenes specials, in combination with music videos.

During and after 2003, many new rock and hip-hop shows were introduced, including specials featuring artists such as Madonna and the return of *Headbangers Ball*, the latter being composed basically of hard rock and heavy metal. Of particular note was Madonna's controversial "Erotica" video, which was voted into the number one spot. MTV2 played the video, which was originally banned on regular MTV, uncensored and in its entirety, and this was instrumental in re-emphasizing that MTV2 hadn't lost its "alternative" and "edgy" quality.

In the summer of 2004 the programming moved on to mostly repeats of MTV's documentaries and reality shows. Little in the way of music video programming remained. Another reinvention of MTV2 then arrived as the channel was relaunched.

MTV2's Major Relaunch

MTV2 (in conjunction with MTV) undertook a major preview of its relaunch with a new identity at the half-time break during Super Bowl XXXIX on February 6, 2005. MTV2 now focused on the males aged 12 to 34 years segment.

The relaunch of the channel was accompanied by a new MTV2 logo—a two-headed dog—in place of the famous MTV block logo. The implication was that the new channel would be nothing like the current MTV. At the time, *Billboard Radio Monitor* suggested that the two heads of the dog were symbolic of rock and hip-hop, the two sides of MTV2.

In an attempt to appear more "edgy" and "cool" to its target audience, MTV2 added video clips from old B-movies, as well as others from the Internet and some created in-house, in between normal video rotation, commercial breaks, and at the top of each hour. These clips serve as station IDs for the new MTV2 and are intended to convey the channel's "anything goes" attitude.

Essentially, however, the relaunch was mainly cosmetic, as the fundamental programming changes had already taken place. The initial aim of the channel—to be a continuous mix of music videos—had disappeared and all the changes described above, plus many more too numerous to mention, mean that MTV2 is now totally different to the MTV2 that started up in 1996. Nevertheless, MTV2 has succeeded in balancing innovation and change with the consistency of the brand promise, and remains close to the MTV core values of the brand.

VHl

VH1–the name originally stood for "Video Hits 1"–was created in 1985 by Warner-Amex Satellite Entertainment Company and then bought by Viacom, the owner of MTV Networks and the MTV brand. At that time, VH1's aim was to target the older crowd of MTV's 18–35-years target audience who preferred lighter, softer kinds of popular music, such as Sting, Billy Joel, and Elton John.

In 1994, VH1 reinvented itself as VH1: Music First and began to shift its focus from broadcasting just music videos to more music-related and lifestyle shows. However, it didn't differentiate itself enough from the stronger MTV brand and almost went under because of poor ratings and the resultant fall in revenues. However, in the fall of 1996, things began to change when it aired an "innovative" show called *Pop Up Video*, which offered snips of information as the music videos were being played. "Pop-up" television took off, and many shows, including *The Drew Carey Show, Sabrina the Teenage Witch,* and even a special episode of *Who Wants To Be A Millionaire?*, had "pop-up" content.

In 1998, VH1 debuted its first annual *VH1 Divas* concert, the format of an annual show similar to MTV's music awards but with the aim of preserving and enhancing music education in local schools through VH1's Save the Music Foundation. The show was well received, and the Foundation celebrated its tenth year in 2007.

In the early 2000s, VH1 changed its format again and returned to playing more mainstream videos. Music artists such as Eminem, Jay-Z, and Missy Elliott began to appear on VH1, which focused on making its content entertaining. In line with this, the channel began to target the pop culture nostalgia market–focusing on the 1980s and 1990s, and collections of "The Greatest," "The Most Shocking," and "The Most Awesomely Bad" videos. Many other changes in programming were seen from 2002 onwards.

While VH1 still plays videos, it is basically like MTV with reality-based music programming featuring shows such as *Behind the Music*, with its focus on pop culture. Also like MTV, it has specific channels for specific countries, such as Australia, Brazil, Europe, India, and Indonesia. But again, as with MTV2, these innovative activities in VH1's programming dialed up and reinforced the brand personality characteristics of *risky, bold, passionate, open, unpredictable, and no bullshit.*

mtvU

MTV created mtvU in order to target viewers who are concerned with issues such as career, activism, and education. *think* MTV also materialized to appeal to a highly intelligent viewer audience. mtvU provides us with another example of how innovation and the use of brand personality are blended to extend the brand.

Formerly College Television Network (CTN), mtvU is a TV channel of MTV networks that caters to college and university campuses across the United States. Usually, TV monitors are strategically placed in student centers or student union buildings, especially in the cafeteria or games room. It originally began as a venture to install video jukeboxes at these locations. Today, it is a broadband channel available to college students at the click of a mouse button in their college dorms.

mtvU is dedicated to aspects of college life, including music (establishing itself yet again as the music authority figure), news (stimulating), and on-campus events (Madonna as a stand-in professor, tailgate tour with barbecues, pep rallies, and homecoming parades) that flex the brand values of "weird quotient" and "humorous." These events constantly create a "buzz" around campuses. mtvU's team of VJs also travel the country visiting campuses, meeting students, and bringing them the latest events. In essence, mtvU has positioned itself among a certain segment of its target audience, providing a variety of opportunities to empower and entertain students on-air, online, and on campus.

Although MTV is known as a brash, boundary-pushing network, it has had to tread carefully in Asia. MTV Asia reaches 134 million households in the region that encompasses Southeast

Asia, China, India, South Korea, and the Philippines. Each of these markets has its own unique culture and character, to which MTV must be sensitive while at the same time preserving its edgy core values. As Frank Brown, MTV Asia's former president, once commented: "We think of our consumers as dual-passport holders: they wear sneakers and baseball caps but are equally comfortable in traditional dress with their families. There's a common bond among young people today that there has never been for any past generation, and MTV provides them with a wonderful window to the rest of the world."

To keep all target audiences happy and ratings high, brands like MTV have to keep all their products fresh and relevant. This means constant evolution of product offerings and brand relevance.

KEEPING THE PRODUCTS FRESH

What you have read so far will leave you in no doubt that MTV frequently and in different ways uses speed, flexibility, and innovation in order to keep its brand fresh. Its pace of innovation and change is staggering, and it has been a challenge to keep up with the brand changes while writing this book. However, all the changes still rotate around the central brand values.

Since MTV first came up with its famous campaign slogan, "I want my MTV," the network has had to keep up with ever-changing teen trends in order to keep its product offerings fresh. Tim Brooks, co-author of *The Complete Directory to Prime Time, Network, and Cable TV Shows*, said: "These young people live in today, and that means being eternally hip and contemporary."[2]

Ideas are generated in-house by people who are connected to the pop culture and the latest music. MTV seldom uses out-of-house creatives. This is partly due to the constant need to make changes, which would make it difficult to keep an agency updated at all times. Projects are managed from conception of ideas to production, generally in under two weeks. To facilitate this process, an inclusive approach is taken to ideas generation within the global network of MTV.

The strong relationship which MTV has with its audience ensures that new ideas also come from viewers themselves. Viewers partner with MTV to bring out the best in its shows, and to provide it with suggestions as to the kinds of shows they want to see.

Another way to keep the product fresh is to connect music with young people's experiences. In MTV's *Pick and Play*, viewers are given the opportunity to choose a special time in their lives and select a song that they associate with it. In other words, MTV helps teens create a soundtrack of their lives. In this way, MTV constantly uses different angles and adopts new ways to give young people a platform for expressing themselves.

Programs are also kept fresh by being tied to different brands or businesses that not only help to create the show, but also offer prizes to be won. For example, with one promotion, a viewer could win a Sony Ericsson W800i Walkman Phone if the song they have voted for appeared on MTV's *Pick and Play*. Young people are quick to realize that they stand to gain a lot by being involved.

In general, it is MTV's inherent values—its willingness, despite its size, to take risks and to explore new ideas—plus its reverence for non-conformity and its up-to-the-minute understanding of what is going on in pop culture, that keep its product offerings fresh.

LOCAL (COUNTRY) RELEVANCE AND PROGRAMMING AUTONOMY

MTV's local country relevance isn't limited to its programming/content; the staff who produce the shows, the VJs, and even the president of each channel, are local people.

MTV's strength has always derived from its versatility, and from being able to reflect back at its billion or so viewers their national identity, hopes, dreams, fears, and desires. No matter where in the world you live, what your skin color is, or what faith you believe in, it is guaranteed that you will be able to relate to MTV. As discussed in previous chapters, in India this means soap operas and Bollywood numbers, mixed with episodes of the homegrown version of *Punk'd*, called *MTV Bakra*. In Italy, music bands drop by the MTV studio to whip up their favorite dishes in an on-set kitchen. Brazilian VJs star as the superpowered heroes of their own animated series, *Megaliga*.

MTV Indonesia, which broadcasts to the most populous Muslim country in the world, pauses five times a day so that viewers are reminded to pray. Instead of customizing some of the more scandalous offerings broadcast in other parts of the world, MTV Indonesia celebrates the month-long festival of religious observance, Ramadan, and manages to make it look "cool" for its viewers.

Once a local MTV channel is seen as a pop cultural icon, it will begin to shed its foreignness. Operations are decentralized and managed locally. At MTV India, local Indians run their channel independently, managing everything from the profit and loss statements to the creative content. This process encourages the generation of ideas from all over the world, which can then be picked up by other MTV networks.

The offices of MTV's Japanese, Korean, and Thai channels—all of which have been broadcasting only since 2001—are located in Tokyo, Seoul, and Bangkok, respectively. MTV Base, the first channel in Africa, began life in London but moved to South Africa in October 2006. More examples of localization are described in Chapter 10, where the country cases of China and India are discussed in detail.

This chapter has focused on how MTV is managing its brand in line with the expectations and wants of its customers. Brand management and guardianship are of pivotal importance if any brand is to be successful, and a systematic approach to this is given below.

BRAND MANAGEMENT AND GUARDIANSHIP

The key to successful brand management is to try and manage all the touchpoints that the brand has with its customers. This can be depicted in diagrammatic form, and in Figures 9.1 and 9.2 you will see examples of general and specific brand management wheel diagrams. "Brand guardianship" is a term used to describe how a brand is managed systematically.

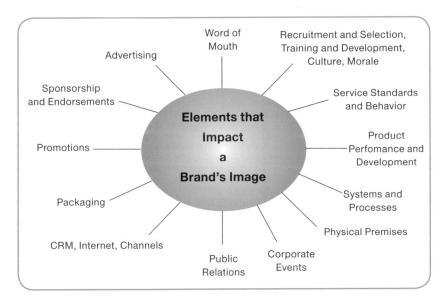

Figure 9.1 **The Generic Brand Management Wheel**

In many of the world's top branded companies today, the responsibility for guarding the brand is usually lodged with the top management team, or a specifically dedicated committee or board, who are ultimately responsible for managing strategic brand activities and ensuring that all aspects of the brand's activities reinforce the brand vision, values, and personality. It is imperative that all brand initiatives follow the brand strategy, and consistently and positively influence consumers' experiences with and perceptions of the brand.

Brand guardianship also ensures that there is buy-in and commitment from everyone within the organization, and thus it shapes corporate behavior. The "brand guardian," whether one person or several people, tries to guard every consumer touchpoint. Typically, the brand management wheel depicts the many areas of activity that need to be controlled to ensure that everything that can impact on the consumer experience remains well managed and that, as a consequence, the brand image is consistently good.

The MTV Brand Management Wheel

MTV's brand management wheel looks like Figure 9.2 and includes elements such as roadshows, outdoor events, contests, and promotions, which have to be managed and checked regularly to ensure they are not "off-brand." MTV manages its brand by separating out the tasks. For example, content being the major consumer touchpoint, much of MTV's content may originate from one central location, such as MTV Networks International headquarters in London. At the same time, by applying its "think global, act local" strategy, local countries are empowered to generate additional programming and brand marketing activities across the brand management wheel to provide a sense of ownership and relevance. This sounds easy, but it is difficult to get the balance right.

Throughout this book, reference has been made to many of the brand management wheel components that MTV has to control and evolve over time. Two areas that have not yet been examined in detail are co-branding and the MTV culture.

Co-branding

Co-branding, sometimes called "cross-platform marketing," is a popular means of developing new approaches in order to reach target audiences that are currently customers of another brand. It is also a useful way of sharing marketing costs with partners. For instance, in 2003 when Motorola signed a three-year, US$75 million deal with MTV International, the aim of the marketing collaboration was to target a new set of customers that Motorola hadn't previously tapped, while allowing MTV to tap into Motorola's existing customer base, which hadn't previously been penetrated by MTV. Motorola brings MTV's programming to a wireless, mobile platform through its devices. The two companies have created integrated marketing activities such as *MTV Motoalert*, which brings the target audience closer to their favorite artists.

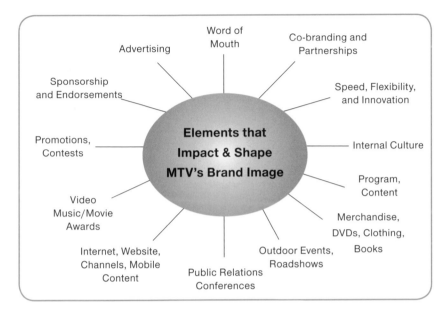

Figure 9.2 The MTV Brand Management Wheel

For example, when Marion Raven visited Malaysia, hundreds of Motorola users were advised of her showcase at a prestigious Kuala Lumpur hotel. While watching Raven on stage, fans could also see the banners of sponsors for the showcase, which included Motorola and MTV.

Another reason for co-branding is to provide additional benefits to MTV's own customer base while at the same time enhancing brand loyalty. For example, MTV's co-branding with Motorola provides its loyal customers with games, downloadable themes, packaged wallpaper, screensavers, ringtones from MTV artists, programming segments, music and concert information, and special promotions. Motorola owners who are fans of MTV could get MTV content on their phone. In fact, MTV leaves no co-branding stone unturned. In June 2005, Malaysia's second-largest telecommunications provider, DiGi, teamed up with MTV to provide its target audience (secondary and tertiary students) with mobile prepaid packages with MTV programming/content at a bargain price.

MTV has also ventured into the co-branding of credit cards. In India in 2001, the MTV Citibank Card launched in association with MasterCard was specifically designed to address the lifestyle aspirations of "youth" and the "young-at-heart."[3] More recently, in the Philippines, MTV launched the MTV Card, a co-branded card between MTV and Equitable CardNetwork, Inc. that is "designed to address the lifestyle and interests of today's MTV Generation— clubbing, cravings, fashion, entertainment, indulgence, escapades, gadgets and other things important to young people."[4]

Also in 2007, Malaysia's Hong Leong Bank relaunched its MTV Credit Card in order to tap the potential 2.5 million "emerging young professionals" segment. Approximately 50,000 new cardholders were expected to join in 2007.[5] The bank's group managing director, Yvonne Chia, explained that the exclusive tie-up with MTV would help to revitalize the bank's image and increase its appeal to the younger generation. "The card offers music, fashion, food, travel and entertainment benefits and privileges to young and hip professionals aged between 24 and 32 years and earning over RM24,000 a year," she said.

In terms of what makes a suitable co-branding relationship, other companies may wish to follow MTV's lead, and do as follows:

1. Ensure that your customers will receive real benefits/ "perks" from the co-branding exercise.

2. Ensure that the target audiences of the partners have similar demographic and psychographic profiles. For instance, DiGi's prepaid customers in Malaysia are mostly school students aged 15 and over.

3. Ensure that the partners have similar brand values to facilitate working together strategically. For instance, McDonald's and MTV launched a global music partnership to strengthen their connection with young adult audiences through an exclusive program called *Advance Warning*.

McDonald's popular "I'm lovin' it" campaign builds on the company's strong connection to young adults' passions—music, entertainment, sports, and fashion. This is similar to MTV's values of connecting to young adults with similar passions.

4. Ensure that the brand partner doesn't eclipse your own brand name. Co-branding should emphasize and elevate both brand names. At the 2005 launch by Philips and MTV of season three of *MTV Whatever Things*, neither brand "eclipsed" the other. Instead, the wacky, witty, stunt-oriented show used Philips' products in the stunts performed on the program. Arshit Pathak, general manager of Wireless, Consumer Electronics, Philips India Limited, said of this collaboration between MTV and Philips that the two companies share a similar mindset, and that the collaboration cements their commitment to empower today's youth to do the things that matter most to them in their own way, through stylish and intuitively designed innovations that form the essential things in their lives. In other words, Philips, through *MTV Whatever Things*, celebrates the spontaneity of youth.

The final aspect of brand management that stands out significantly is the culture of the MTV organization. MTV is widespread across the globe, yet it still manages to have the same kind of mindset and culture among all its employees.

Living within the MTV Culture

The MTV brand is lived out and cultivated by the many people behind the scenes who have created and brought the brand to where it is today. As a brand exists only in the consumer's mind, every contact with consumers can potentially be a moment of truth. Everyday moments, whether positive or negative, can either strengthen or lessen the emotional bond that brands such as MTV have with their target audiences.

Bringing the brand to life involves every function in the company, and every consumer touchpoint; as such, it is no easy task. Usually, if a company has a clear brand strategy, then it is much easier to manage the consumer touchpoints. The brand strategy includes knowing where the brand is heading, what the brand personality is, and the positioning of the brand compared to its competitors. Without all this, it is impossible for a brand to be consistent. The result is usually a confused, mixed, and relatively poor brand image, with those responsible for that image coming under fire when ratings are perceived to be poor.

The way the MTV brand is lived out is seen in the way the company employs its people and by the way in which they make decisions that affect the brand. Since the brand is a beacon to young people, and has to be seen as irreverent, MTV allows decisions to be made from the bottom up, from the grass-roots level, so that the most innovative ideas often come from creative people in the lower ranks. The company regularly looks out for young talent, and tolerates a high level of turnover in the creative department, in order to get the freshest, most innovative people and ideas. In today's competitive environment, innovation is a "must have"—and MTV shows the way.

CONCLUSION

The MTV brand is undoubtedly a global success, and much of that success is due to the apparent control of the brand through brand management. While not appearing to possess strict brand guardianship structures and guidelines in the orthodox way of many top brands (brand management committees, etc.), MTV nevertheless manages its brand well across all markets. It has succeeded in the difficult task of keeping brand consistency while at the same time exhibiting constant innovation in terms of product and managing all customer touchpoints.

The future challenge for MTV lies in managing the brand in the digital world, as discussed in Chapter 11. Meanwhile, the next chapter looks at MTV India and MTV China to see how the brand is managed in these two very different countries and cultures.

1 Jeff Yang, "Asian Pop: Channeling Asian America—Six new 24-hour TV channels go after the hearts, minds and eyeballs of English-speaking Asians in the U.S.," *SFGate.com*, February 2, 2005, http://www.sfgate.com/cgi-bin/article.cgi?file=/gate/archive/2005/02/02/asiaTV.DTL.

2 Tim Brooks and Earle F. Marsh, *The Complete Directory to Prime Time, Network, and Cable TV Shows: 1946-Present*, 7th ed. (New York: Ballantine Books, 1999).

3 Press release: "MTV and Citibank launch India's first credit card for the youth," April 27, 2001, www.citigroup.com, http://www.citigroup.com/citigroup/press/2001/010427a.htm.

4 The MTV Credit Card by Equitable Card, http://www.equitablecard.com/mtv/mtvcredit/faq.htm.

5 "HL Bank eyes over 50,000 users of MTV Credit Card," *www.bernama.com*, January 30, 2007, http://www.bernama.com.my/bernama/v3/printable.php?id=244164.

MTV Shows
Music Videos Be on MTV
Live Performances Downloads Artist Photos Genres
Shop MTV Shows Show Photos
Europe Music Awards MTV Shows Gossip
Shop
mtv

Brand-Building Case Studies: MTV India and MTV China

10

The emphasis in this book has been on MTV in Asia, while giving relevant information about MTV's roots and activities in the United States and Europe. This chapter presents two detailed case studies on how MTV in Asia has penetrated—and developed and managed its brand in—the world's two fastest-growing economies with huge youth markets—namely, MTV India and MTV China.

CASE STUDY I: MTV INDIA

Youth is now driving the economy of India, and will continue to do so. Approximately 54% of India's one billion people are under 25 years of age, and 600 million (approximately 10% of the world's population) are under 28—right in the target range of MTV. These figures are expected to grow. In fact, India accounts for 20% of worldwide births, with one baby being born every two seconds. Future projections of the youth population are therefore substantial.

MTV started in India as MTV Asia in 1991, but MTV India is now an autonomous channel. In an interview with *agencyfaqs!*, former managing director of MTV India, Alex Kuruvilla, commented that an MTV survey conducted in 1991 had found that 60% of all young people in India at that time thought MTV was the "coolest" television channel.[1] MTV's immense potential in India has only increased in the intervening years. Things haven't changed a lot in terms of MTV's popularity, but MTV has made fundamental changes in India, as indeed it has globally, as market dynamics and customer needs change.

MTV India has a tradition of reaching young people not only through music videos, but also with programs dealing with social issues such as the plight of rural Indian youth, poverty generally, and problems of child labor, child prostitution, and street children. Despite the polarization of poverty and privilege in India, research indicates that every class, regardless of its circumstances, feels optimistic about the future.

Youth in general have similar attitudes in India as in other countries around the world: they like to be fashionable, to be who they want to be, to try new things, and generally to explore themselves and their talents. But within these generalities, different segments are evident.

An interesting fact is that the Indian youth market is far from being homogeneous. The Indian Market Research Bureau study entitled *Tuning into the Indian Youth, Part 3*, conducted in 2001, divides the youth market into the following segments:

- homebodies (16%)
- two-faced–inwardly traditional, outwardly modern (16%)
- wannabes–materialistic show-offs (25%)
- rebels (23%)
- cool guys–the influencers (20%).[2]

Indian youths, at the time of the study, revealed that they are aggressive, independent, and highly competitive, and while they might still respect their parents and not retaliate when rebuked by them, they wouldn't see any problem with placing their parents in a retirement home for the aged. This is apparently a common attitude, even among the homebodies. Their main aims in life are to be financially successful, and to have fun.

India: Fertile Ground for MTV

India is a country of many juxtapositions and contrasts. Tom Freston, former CEO of MTV Networks, described India as an exhilarating country, filled with surprise and wonder, excitement mixed with chaos and commotion–a country where one sees the past mixed with the present, such as Bollywood movies vying for audiences with American reality TV shows and cable TV networks such as ESPN.

MTV targeted India because of its huge potential. In 2004, MTV India was making only about US$25 million a year, an insignificant amount compared to the US$27 billion a year generated by Viacom, MTV's parent company. MTV India is "mostly about the future, and the future looks bright," Freston said in 2004.[3]

The key to MTV India's success all along has been that it manages to reflect the local culture, despite being originally a Western brand. Most people in India are poor, living on less than US$200 a year; yet the country has a growing middle-class population (around 300 million) who wear fashionable clothes and drive cars. The economy has been growing well every year, and is touted as one of the fastest-growing, free market economies in Asia after China. People are beginning to acquire material items that they could never have afforded in the past, such as mobile phones and TV sets. India also continues to grow at a rapid pace in several sectors, such as healthcare, tourism, and the information technology outsourcing industry, which has seen the United States and European countries looking to India for this kind of expertise.

India's Media Landscape

With regards to the media industry, cable has become one of India's most dynamic and growing businesses, with the number of subscribers growing by about 20% a year and advertising revenues growing by about 10% annually, although from a small base since it is a less mature industry. In a *Fortune* article on MTV, India was described as "a country that enjoys robust democracy, a boisterous press, and a vibrant film and music industry."[4] All the global entertainment giants—Disney, Sony, Time Warner, Discovery Communications, NBC—whose businesses have prospered in the United States and in Western Europe have expanded into India and the rest of Asia in search of growth and new opportunities. For instance, Disney launched its Disney Channel in India in 2004.

The media landscape in India is rather fragmented and dense; and while cable network operators abound, new channels and broadcasters continue to enter the already saturated industry. Cable operators are forming alliances to consolidate funds and streamline their operations in order to equip the country with up-to-date communications infrastructure. While the TV market in India still has a lot of potential for growth, a new feature of the media industry is direct-to-home satellite businesses. Cable television viewing is fast becoming an expensive proposition, because more and more broadcasters are charging for their channels.

Even MTV initially existed as a free-to-air (FTA) channel, but converted to a pay channel within two years of entering the Indian market. The basis for a pay channel is to recover part of its manufacturing costs. However, Telecom Regulatory Authority of India (TRAI) issued an order in October 2004 that prevents broadcasters from hiking their subscription rates for existing channels. However, multi-systems operators (MSOs—middlemen who take signals from broadcasters and pass them on to local operators) have the problem of trying to capitalize on the growth opportunities provided by pay channels, while facing resistance from customers over rising subscription prices. The situation in India is such that it has the lowest average revenue per user in the world.

MTV India's Competition

MTV entered India in 1991 by licensing a music channel designed for all of Asia to Star TV, which dealt with the local cable "wallahs" who sold the ads on the channel and shared the revenue with MTV. When News Corp. bought Star TV in 1993, MTV went solo, while Star TV started the Indian music channel now known as Channel V, in competition with MTV.

By late 2003, it was apparent that MTV was doing much better than its competitors such as CNN or anything owned by Rupert Murdoch (see Figure 10.1). Since then, competition for MTV has

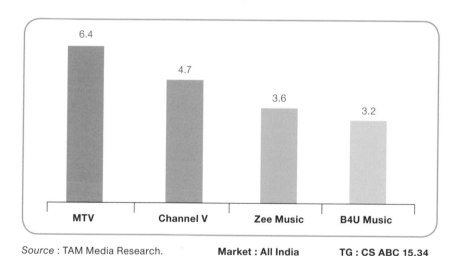

Source : TAM Media Research.   Market : All India   TG : CS ABC 15.34

Figure 10.1 Average Weekly Reach of MTV Channels, September 21 to October 18, 2003 (millions of viewers)

remained tough in India. For instance, most families own only one TV set; therefore, watching TV becomes a joint family affair and only one channel can be watched at any one time. MTV then has to compete with the other entertainment channels, as well as news and sport. For example, in 2002, the top-rated TV show in India was a soap opera on Murdoch's channel Star Plus whose title, translated into English, was *The Mother-in-Law was Once the Daughter-in-Law*. Channel surfing is also seldom an option; which makes it even harder for MTV, since its programs are tailored to let viewers catch on even if they tune in part-way through a program.

MTV's key direct competitors in India are Channel V, Zee Music, and B4U music. In addition, there are numerous regional channels playing music videos, 24 hours a day, in local languages. India has 18 officially recognized spoken languages, but within those are about 200 different mother tongues. This poses complex problems of segmentation for the music business.

Staying on Top of the Game

Both MTV and Channel V claim to be the number one music channel in India. Some find little to distinguish between them, so how loyal are their viewers? How do these channels garner and retain the interest of viewers?

Atul Phadnis of TAM Media Research in India admits that the music channels' market shares are pretty low. For music channels to grow, he says, a key requirement is innovation and the building of specific associations. Others say that differentiation comes in the form of packaging and presentation styles, VJs, and non-music shows such as challenges, contests, and travel-related programs. So, how do the different channels compare and differentiate?

Channel V points to one of its reality shows, *Pop Stars*, a "bite viewing" type of show that differs from the traditional appointment viewing patterns. For Zee Music, it's "more music and less *bak bak* [a Hindi word for "meaningless chatter"]."[5] They play full songs, instead of the 30-/60-second clips basically promoting forthcoming Bollywood movies. MTV points to shows such as *MTV*

Youth Icon, Lycra MTV Style Awards (where MTV invites advertisers to help develop the program), *MTV Roadies*, and *MTV IMMIES*. Furthermore, MTV says it differentiates itself through its VJs, such as Cyrus Broacha, famous for playing pranks on celebrities and well-known athletes on *MTV Bakra*, a customized *Candid Camera* for local Indians. Broacha and the program are so popular that friends of Bollywood stars and famous cricket players contact MTV specifically to request Broacha to play a *bakra* on the celebrity. Even MTV's competitors agree that Broacha is able to relate to and connect with young audiences.

MTV India learnt early on that in order to stay on top of the game, it couldn't just sell MTV (America) wholesale to local Indians, because India isn't just one market but many. There are different types of viewers, speaking different languages. MTV had to respond creatively. It started to include local Bollywood videos along with its American programming in order to suit the tastes of local Indian teenagers. It placed itself in the heart of the entertainment industry in India, with its offices located in Mumbai, launched its own 24-hour channel, and localized its programs in order to compete with Star TV's Channel V. Bill Roedy admits that MTV had to drive deep into the culture in order to overtake Channel V and become India's top-rating music channel. MTV India has had to reinvent itself constantly, with programs such as *MTV Ek Do Teen, MTV Tech Check, MTV Roadies, Baap of Baakra*, *MTV Big Picture*, and the interactive *MTV Kya Baat Hai*, and with new VJs such as Piddhu The Great and Aila! Tendulka.

The critical aspect in turning a product that was 100% international into one with almost entirely local content was to base the product on consumer research and insight. MTV decided who was its target market—who it wanted to serve—then researched that particular audience to find out what made them tick. For example, when MTV India launched a daily soap opera, it was considered a "bold" move. The strategy proved to be very successful, and it came from an insight that revealed young people as heavy soap opera viewers. However, Frank Brown, former president of MTV

Networks Asia, acknowledged that there were some lessons to be learnt from crafting soap operas for the MTV target audience, in terms of keeping them youth-focused and true to the MTV brand.

Another way in which MTV displays a keen insight into the Indian market is by coming up with program hits, such as the previously mentioned *MTV Bakra*. MTV has put together a think tank of programmers, split between New York and London, who come up with about a dozen concepts designed for global consumption. However, MTV India still partners with local content providers to produce innovative programs.

Advertising Dollars

Besides facing issues of cultural preferences with programming, MTV India faces a tough battle and strong competition with regards to making money from advertising. The media market as a whole is highly fragmented, not just the music market with its various genres. There are too many cable TV operators and networks, resulting in the annual advertising spend of around US$600 million being stretched too thinly among them. Prior to a wave of consolidations in 2004, there were about 50,000 cable operators. The number was reduced to around 25,000 operators, serving 50 million subscribers—about half of all the homes with a TV set. Subscribers pay only about US$3 a month for cable, leaving pennies for the networks.

Even though MTV is well known as a catalyst for understanding and reaching the young people of today, the struggle for advertising dollars is very much a reality for the network. "With so many sellers of commercials, MTV cannot command premium prices for advertising, even on its popular shows. Media buyers say that a prime-time 30-second spot on MTV typically sells for roughly US$175 to US$250, while daytime spots are even cheaper!"[6]

MTV has responded creatively with several initiatives aimed at going beyond the selling of 30-second spots. First, it invites advertisers to help it develop new programs. Second, it has centralized its sales operations team, setting up global and regional sales teams to sell ads to multinational companies. MTV has thus become a one-stop shop for companies to place ads for the entire world. For example, in 2003 Motorola made a three-year US$75 million commitment to buy commercials on MTV in Europe, Latin America, and Asia. Third, MTV has expanded its target audience to include a slightly older cohort by tailoring its programs to hold their attention for longer. Instead of going with their usual media consumption model for the United States, similar to "snacking," it has moved its audience to a more regular appointment viewing with programs such as the daily soap opera *It's a Beautiful Life*, a youth-oriented series that proved so popular its original 39 episodes were extended to more than 100. Fourth, it started collecting subscriber fees for the network and joined the Sony-backed group of channels known as One Alliance. Fifth, MTV has entered into entirely new lines of business to boost its earnings, such as selling merchandise ranging from MTV-branded fragrances and CDs, to a whole set of stylish clothing, and bringing out an MTV credit card, co-branded with Citigroup. MTV India has also started exporting some of its programming to cable and satellite operators in the United Kingdom, the Middle East, and the Caribbean, in a bid to reach the Indian diaspora.

Finally, a viable strategy to increase ad revenues is to form strategic alliances such as the past partnership with TATA Indicom, part of the huge TATA conglomerate, that included ad buys, sponsorships, and co-branded mobile phones.

In conclusion, cable operators are still signing up new subscribers, and advertising is growing at a double-digit pace despite the tightness that still exists as a result of dividing available advertising dollars among the plethora of cable networks. Still, the advertising expenditure pie is getting larger. MTV doesn't mind waiting; it's a business that has a long-term perspective.

MTV India's Innovation, Programming, and Community Building

Innovation

One of MTV's global drivers for everything that they do is to promote interactive entertainment for new platforms. In line with that, in July 2005, MTV India launched four new programs promoting mobile interactivity. This is in line with its target audience, who are avid users of the Internet and mobile phones. These four programs operate in "real time," allowing viewers to use their mobile phones to react to what they see on the screen, as well as to communicate with other viewers instantaneously. This is cutting-edge programming. These new developments in India indicated MTV Networks' focus on digital media, as well as on India as a key market in the space. India is only the third market after Japan and Korea to launch mobile interactivity.

The four shows launched were *Doctor Love, Love Letter, Bol Baby Poll,* and *Ha Ya Na.* In *Doctor Love,* viewers sent a text message to the show, asking a question about their personal love relationship; an instant reply is flashed on the screen. In *Love Letter,* viewers sent a text message to the show to get their own customized love letter to a loved one shown on screen. *Bol Baby Poll* featured a new topic every day for viewers to vote on, giving them a voice on any topic. Finally, *Ha Ya Na* featured music videos determined by viewer votes.

Programming

MTV India has won more than 60 national and international awards, including PROMAX 2005 Golds for Best Promotional Campaign (*MTV IMMIES)* and Best Programming Package (*MTV IMMIES*), PROMAX Asia 2004 Golds for Best Entertainment Programme Promo (*Yaarana Gharana*), Best Sound Design (*MTV IMMIES*), and Funniest Spot (*Tele Shopping-Hand),* and Silver for Style Awards, among others.

Wacky signature shows such as *MTV Bakra, MTV Fully Faltoo*, and *MTV Liftman*, as well as on-air promos featuring celebrities such as Bill Gates and Colin Powell, have elevated the brand to its premier status. MTV India has evolved into a 360-degree brand by launching the Asian Bankers award-winning MTV Citibank Credit Card and MTV Style clothing and accessories. Youth-oriented programs such as the VJ Hunt now incorporate text message voting by viewers, to make them feel more involved in the competitions. Viewers can also download updates on their favorite local and international music, celebrities, and lifestyle programs on their mobile phones.

MTV India has also set a Guinness World Record with the World's Longest Dance Party, as well as introducing India's largest-scale interactive television, text message, and online voting, and VJ and movie talent hunts. MTV India also reaches a wider audience via hugely successful events such as the Youth Marketing Forum, the most insightful and sought-after events for the marketing community, with its focus on reaching that critical mass of the Millennials, the Lycra MTV Style Awards, and the MTV IMMIES—the ultimate Indian Music Excellence awards.

Finally, *It's a Beautiful Life* showcased the talents of six young people who were discovered after a country-wide talent hunt conducted by MTV. It was MTV India's first foray into youth fiction, making their programming content always fresh.

Community Building

MTV is reputed to be in the leadership position in the Indian entertainment scenario because of the impact it has had on Indian youth, especially through its pro-social work in the area of HIV/AIDS. The "MTV Music Summit for AIDS" and "Staying Alive" stood out as the premier, youth-focused AIDS awareness initiatives in India. Such accolades have made MTV India one of the four most successful MTV brands across the world, according to a global equity study. The third "MTV Music Summit for AIDS" was held in Mumbai on November 15, 2003 for 35,000 fans, and featured appearances by MTV India's VJs, Bollywood stars such as Dino Morea, Dia Mirza, and Fardeen Khan, and Indian music acts such as Abhijeet, Babul Supriyo, Baba Sehgal, and DJ Aqeel. (The 2004 to 2006 shows were held in the Philippines.) The event was produced in partnership with United Nations Development Programme (UNDP), and presented by Sony Hi-Fi, with TATA Indicom as the communication partner. The special premiered on both MTV India and Doordarshan, India's public television broadcaster, on November 30 of that year and was watched in 80 million homes.

Despite enjoying considerable success, MTV has had to move on in order to keep up with changing times and lifestyles and to keep revenues climbing, culminating in a major repositioning exercise in 2007.

MTV India's 2007 Repositioning

By September 2007, MTV India had undergone a new positioning exercise, another example of the brand's constant evolution and innovation. The repositioning wasn't just confined to creating new shows, although 14 new programs and seven revamped ones will be gradually introduced. Promotions such as Silky Kumar and shows like *iSuperstar* are typical of a brand-new programming line-up that is very Bollywood-oriented.

A new VJ (Mia), a rejuvenated website, and plans for mobile initiatives, along with fresh graphics, have produced a new look for MTV that MTV India's general manager and vice president–creative and content, Ashish Patil, claims is "slick, young and fresh."[7]

But MTV still demonstrates its concern for relevance–for example, in terms of the needs and concerns of the countries in which it operates. This is typified by the program *Sold*, which is the lead feature of the "MTV Exit" campaign that aims to raise awareness of and help prevent human trafficking. *Sold* is a documentary campaign produced in partnership with the US Agency for International Development (USAID), and premiered in Mumbai in September 2007.

Audience Focus

The target audience is as per the usual demographics mentioned throughout this book. MTV India's target for communications is young people aged 15–24 and a media deliveries target of ages 12–24, but the key focus is the 18–21 age bracket. According to Patil, this is the crowd that is constantly changing in terms of defining what is "cool" and fun. They are fickle and constantly evolving themselves. Patil sums them up as "invincible and fragile," and "emotional and insecure," and describes their motto as: "It's my life, it's my world." Here he sees a distinct resemblance to the philosophy and evolution of MTV itself.[8] In India, Patil says, young people are looking not only for music but also "gaming, romance, dating, travel, adventure, food, relationships, the works!" However, music remains the core of the MTV offering, occupying around 70% of content.[9]

The Results?

Although the newly positioned MTV has yet to be evaluated, MTV currently has a 40% market share, according to Ashish Patil. Revenue is up 40% on 2006, and advertising yield has grown by 30%.

Conclusion

Although MTV India has faced intrinsic challenges in the past, such as low revenues and limited "channel surfing" opportunities leading to lower numbers of viewers, it has overcome these challenges by seeking new ways to reach out to its viewers in an age of digitalization, and by creating innovative programs, together with an improved range of brand marketing activities and promotions to attract more advertising dollars. It has kept a firm grip on the needs and wants of the youth market in India and has reacted accordingly, with an increasing Bollywood focus. MTV's future in India certainly looks bright.

CASE STUDY 2: MTV IN CHINA

Historical Background and MTV's Penetration

There is no doubt that China is a strategic, but relatively untapped market for MTV, as youth shows none of the reticence of past generations in welcoming new relationships and cultures.

Bill Roedy put the enormity of the market opportunity in China in perspective when he stated that China has 393 million mobile phone users, 110 million Internet users, and more technology users under 30 years of age than anywhere else in the world.[10]

Frank Brown, former president of MTV Networks Asia, saw the opportunities in leveraging on Asia's massive young population in order to expand the MTV business. Under Brown's leadership, between 1999 and 2004, eight uniquely programmed music channels were developed, reaching over 110 million households in Asia. Five regional websites were also launched.

The challenge for MTV of reaching out to the youth of mainland China, Taiwan, and Hong Kong has always been complicated by the fact that MTV has two channels, MTV China and MTV Chinese (formerly MTV Mandarin), with some overlapping content. The key thing here is that MTV doesn't treat Chinese consumers as an undifferentiated mass. It is very experienced in market segmentation and understands the different segments among its Chinese markets. For instance, as young Chinese audiences become more nationalistic, MTV is focusing more on localizing its content.

However, there are also growing differences between the 15–24 and 25–34-year age groups. The younger group is more demanding in terms of local content, objecting to too much American and foreign content; whereas the older viewers are indifferent, and more concerned with their careers and their future.

MTV China and MTV Chinese both reach certain provinces in China, while MTV Chinese is also seen in Taiwan, Singapore, South Korea, the Philippines, and Brunei. MTV had originally launched one Mandarin channel for China and Taiwan, but soon discovered that local tastes in music and fashion varied between the two markets.

In 2002, MTV Mandarin reached 60 million homes in China via 40 Chinese cable systems. In 2001, more than 10,000 teens came to Beijing from all over China to audition to become the next VJ on MTV Mandarin. One finalist, who had traveled for 18 hours, was so distraught at losing that MTV offered to let her VJ for a day!

Challenges and the Media Landscape

In the early years, the Chinese government maintained tight control over the media and MTV was limited to between one and four hours of programming a day. Analysts believed that it would be some time before the government would grant 24-hour broadcasting licenses to foreigners, such as MTV, on a nationwide basis. But on April 20, 2003, true to its forecast, MTV became China's first global brand with a 24-hour channel. Launched in Guangdong province, near Hong Kong, the channel provided an additional reach of 1.8 million TV households, with a total viewership of 10 million TV households in China.

MTV in China isn't devoid of its challenges, particularly when situations arise over which it has no control. In 1999, NATO bombed China's embassy in Belgrade the day after CCTV's (the state-owned national TV network) and MTV's *Music Honors* show was held. This global incident delayed MTV's broadcast of the show, because there was no doubt among the Chinese that the United States had influenced NATO and may have been responsible for the bombing. These sensitivities were clearly stated, since MTV's parent company is US-based. CCTV advised MTV Mandarin not to air the show until the situation in Yugoslavia had been "stabilized."

The concept of *guanxi* (personalized networks of influence) is very important if any foreign company wants to thrive in China and form relationships with local companies and government bodies. MTV has been able to establish strong *guanxi*, riding the waves of a 20-year relationship that started with Sumner Redstone, Viacom's chairman and CEO, visiting China at least once a year to foster good *guanxi* with Chinese government ministers. Bill Roedy has been a frequent visitor to China as well, and used to meet regularly with former Chinese leader Jiang Zemin during those times. Roedy has been known to go to great lengths to establish good rapport with the Chinese. Once, during a long dinner with the Chinese cable operators, he had to join in the drinking games and karaoke.

Working with the Chinese can be challenging. One has continually to balance the act of introducing international fashion and fads to a 5,000-year-old country. Despite the younger generation being enamored of the West, they remain loyal to their own roots. Even Li Yifei, who as head of MTV China spent 10 years in the United States and now works for Viacom, still believes in retaining the roots of Chinese culture. She raises her two children in a Chinese context, sends them to a local Chinese school, and speaks to them in Mandarin.

Because MTV China has been established within the media industry, Viacom's MTV has been able to operate in China through joint ventures and strategic alliances. For example, MTV is one of the first foreign broadcasters to be granted a license to develop a production joint venture with Shanghai Media Group. And on April 28, 2005, MTV established a strategic alliance with China Mobile, closing a landmark deal in Shanghai to provide the first branded music service to China Mobile's 200 million-plus subscribers.

This alliance will be in line with MTV's desire to continue its expansion in China. (MTV had previously enjoyed only limited penetration, being permitted to broadcast only in residential areas where foreigners live, such as hotels of at least three stars and in the Pearl River Delta near Hong Kong.) Regulatory restrictions, however, don't apply to the content provided to China Mobile. This alliance also gives MTV a position in the digital and wireless music market in China, as it recently launched its 3G mobile communications systems.

MTV is to provide China Mobile subscribers with downloadable music ringtones, ringback tones, entertainment news, and clips of popular songs. Li Yifei believes that the mobile phone music services will become the biggest revenue pool for MTV, since the broadcasting and program production businesses are subject to tight regulations. This alliance created two new categories for the annual joint awards hosted by MTV and CCTV, the Music Honors awards: Best Wireless Artist and Best Wireless Song.

China's Youth Market

On one of his visits to China, Sumner Redstone commented that a 20-year-old boy from New York has more in common with a young man from China than he does with his own father. Li Yifei agrees, while acknowledging that a cultural divide remains. Her dream and mission is to narrow that divide.

China has a smaller, younger population than India because of its one-child policy, which has contributed to an aging population. Its working-age population will peak by 2015 and then start to shrink because of low fertility rates compared to India. But who are the Chinese youth? Let's first take a look at the Chinese consumer market at large.

It has been claimed that foreign businesses tend to place priority on getting their products out in the market, and on coming up with ideas on how to advertise their products, based very loosely on what they think people in developing nations want to see in their advertisements.[11] However, this method won't work in China, whose consumer market is quickly becoming sophisticated and complex. With 1.3 billion people, about a fifth of the world's population, China is consuming an ever-growing percentage of the world's commodities and products. For example, China consumes 34.8% of the world's cigarettes, 20.1% of mobile phones (it already has the world's biggest base of mobile-phone subscribers, which is expected to near 600 million by 2009), and 23.2% of televisions.

Chinese kids today know more about the world than any other previous generation and they are avid "techies," making ready use of mobile phones, the Internet (findings by Isuppli research agency project that, by the end of 2007, the number of broadband users will be 57 million in China, compared to 54 million in the United States), and electronic gadgets of every sort. They track the latest fashion trends in Tokyo, and swoon over celebrities from Hong Kong and Taiwan, while watching American movies on pirated DVDs. It is fashionable for the upwardly mobile to switch high-end mobile phones every three months, because an old model suggests that one isn't up with the latest fashions.[12]

Gilbert Lee of Research International advises foreign multinationals to play to China's young consumers' yearning for self-expression, individuality, freedom, and physical attractiveness. They want to project themselves as unique, while desiring to make a positive impression on others. They are also creative, opinionated, and keen experimenters.

China's young adults can be segmented accordingly. A detailed study conducted by Grey Global Group and the British Council in 2005 collected data from participants aged 16–39 and living in 30 large cities. The consumer categories were found to be as follows:

- 34% were labeled as "advancers," who are obsessed with their self-image and money.

- 69% of "advancers" are males, and they play a key influence in their families. They are considered the backbone of China's consumer market because of the influence they have over those below them.

- 17% of those sampled are regarded as "experimenters," who are most likely to be the first to buy a PDA with the latest features.

- 11% of those sampled are key target audiences for MTV, because this is the group classified as "young and hip"—the type who want trendy clothes and big brands. They tend to admire the same celebrities as Taiwanese and Hong Kong youth.

Author of *Beijing Doll*, Chun Sue, the 21-year-old high-school dropout who shot to fame in 2003 with her novel recounting her search for love, truth, and the perfect punk band, says that she is obsessed with material things, and spends money like water just to buy a handbag with a fancy brand name. This is the kind of consumer that MTV thrives on. Chun is individualistic, just like two-thirds of young Chinese who prefer to do things themselves, rather than rely on others. Chun has strong views about George Orwell, Henry Miller, and Dostoevsky, and her views are representative of how many of the young people in China think. Seventy-five percent of Chinese youths believe it is important to be well informed, and imperative if one wants to improve one's station in life.

The survey indicates that the Chinese youth market would be well served by a channel such as *think* MTV. Sixty percent of these young adults care more about the environment, social issues, and public interests than do older Chinese. They have often made efforts to protect the environment, while 59% said that they value brands that support charities.

MTV, being a brand that acts global but thinks local, is no doubt aware that two-thirds of young Chinese adults say they are interested in other cultures and in international events, while 52% say they are attracted to the lifestyles of developed nations. Although they say this, Viveca Chan, former chairman and CEO of Grey Global Group China, points out that their lifestyles beg to differ. They are still very much Chinese and localized.[13]

But there are exceptions. Wang Qi, a 19-year-old hip-hop music producer, has an American-style nickname, "Jerzy King." He carries with him a mini-disc player (uncannily, it's not an iPod) loaded with Eminem, P. Diddy, and Fabolous. He wears a white fleece jacket bearing the logo of the Toronto Maple Leafs; and he has a Western Union credit card, express mailed to him from the United

States, which he uses to buy pants online from Foot Locker, along with other American streetwear, which he resells to his Chinese friends. He spends hours each day on the Internet, tracking the latest hip-hop styles.

MTV's competitive strategy—or rather, the differentiating factor for its brand—is that it has to portray itself as a risk-taker, a characteristic that appeals to a surprisingly large number of Chinese young adults. They pride themselves on charting their own paths and not following the pack. Fifty-nine percent of them believe they need to take risks in order to be successful. They are not content to be passive observers. Instead, they want to be part of the action, and to try new things.

A recent survey conducted by public relations company Hill & Knowlton (China), in conjunction with *Seventeen* magazine (China) and Sinomonitor International, set out to identify students' dreams and aspirations, their role models and preferences, and their definition of "cool." The April 2004 "China Cool Hunt" survey polled 1,200 18- to 22-year-old students from 64 universities in Beijing and Shanghai about the who, what, and why of "cool." The survey results showed that 60% reported spending more than US$60 a month on "unessential items"—a huge sum given that the monthly per capita income in those cities averages less than US$250.

The key to understanding the younger generation in China is first to recognize that they are a breed apart from their parents' and grandparents' generations. Everything is different for them. Their parents endured famine and hardship during the Mao Zedong era, while the present generation is experiencing an era of modernization and prosperity. In Beijing and Shanghai, and even in second-tier cities such as Dalian, Chengdu, and Kunming, new shopping complexes, restaurants, highways, and residential developments are springing up each week.

Although most young people don't realize this, they will eventually have to support their entire families when they grow up and start earning an income. Even now, parents are sending their children to elite kindergartens such as the Beijing Intelligence and

Capability Kindergarten, where golf is a mandatory subject. Fees at the school are US$6,000 a year, double the income of the average Beijing household. Parents have high hopes for their children and try to give them the best. Many parents confess that they push their children hard to compensate for the opportunities they themselves never had.

Because of this, the younger generation (aged 16–39 and living in 30 large cities) are very confident about their future. It is as if there is a Chinese version of the American dream that is to be had. Many young Chinese adults are extremely driven and obsessed with getting ahead in life. They are very eager to get plugged in, and to be associated with the business world. To them, this is the real world. They want a good job, and they are willing to do a lot in order to get it, even joining the Communist Party despite not believing in Communism.

Along with their obsession with getting ahead, they are also looking for fun. This is expressed in some who are considered to be rebels. For example, 21-year-old Li Cheng is considered a rebel because he abandoned the academic path, despite coming from a family of scholars and technical specialists in nuclear science. He found his niche as a VJ with MTV's competitor, Channel V. His family disapproves, but Li enjoys the work because of the pay and other benefits, such as putting on a music festival for a crowd of 10,000 people on the outskirts of Shanghai.[14]

Chinese Content, Local Content, and VJs

Pressure from the local audience has caused MTV to tailor content to suit local tastes. The channel's content is 30% Chinese, 30% Hong Kong and Taiwan, and 40% international, and is an excellent example of how well MTV crosses borders with a group of go-getting and gifted VJs to complement their service. The music is also softer and mainstream, rather in the vein of VH1, owing to the musical tastes of Chinese youth, which go beyond their own generation; hence, the phenomenon of modern Chinese artists doing cover versions of hits from the 1970s.

This reversal of the innovative and cutting-edge becoming mainstream, which is what MTV is known for, is an example of the channel's versatility in putting the needs and wants of its viewers before everything else, and in mixing universal youth sensibilities with local tastes. MTV China learnt from MTV India's mistake in failing to do the same when it first entered the market.

Although some popular shows can cross cultural and social groups, and even language barriers, MTV China has to be cautious. For example, Taiwan produces a lot of shows that can cross borders into China as long as there is no underlying political message. Because of political tensions between Beijing and Taipei, even the slightest mention or portrayal of Taiwanese nationalist leader Chiang Kai Shek can cause trouble for the broadcaster.

VJs are the brand's ambassadors. They live out MTV's brand values and are the emotional link to their target audience. Viewers always want to see a reflection of their own culture and values expressed in the people that represent MTV. And it's no different for Chinese viewers. MTV Chinese's VJs come from very diverse backgrounds, driven by MTV's strategy of "think local, act global." For example, Vivian Tang, the host for a short program featuring fashion and pop culture news and interviews, is part Manchurian, part Jewish, part Han. An ancestor, a Jewish astronomer named Tang Ruowang, served under the Qing Dynasty emperor Kang Xi. Tang fell out of favor with the emperor and was imprisoned. After his release, he married a princess but was again imprisoned, for reasons that are not known, for the rest of his life. Following his death, the emperor rehabilitated the family's partial royal status, which meant that Tang's descendents would only be permitted to marry Manchurians. Vivian's great-grandfather was a Jewish trader from Switzerland.

Another example is Li Xia. Born in Xinjiang (a province in west China), the host is a devout Muslim who got into the TV business from hotel management. She worked on several jobs with Sichuan TV, CCTV-e, and Xinjiang TV (where she wrote, produced, hosted, and edited her own show), and then continued her studies at the Beijing Broadcasting Institute. She then joined MTV, and impressed producers from New York to Singapore with her casual, fast-paced style. Like some other VJs with MTV, she creates her own independent show three times a week, featuring entertainment news and commentary. (MTV Asia's VJ Denise Keller does something similar with her Singapore show, *Eye for a Guy*.)

Two other local VJs showing great potential are Zhu Zhu and Wang Hantao. Zhu Zhu currently hosts *MTV English*, where viewers can improve their language skills assisted by pop music videos and movies with English and Chinese subtitles. Wang Hantao is an IT graduate from Zhejiang University and entered MTV via a VJ contest in 2001. He has hosted MTV China's most popular syndicated show, *Tian Lai Cun* (*Music Village*), and the *CCTV–MTV Music Honors* program.

MTV's Shining Star: Li Yifei

One cannot think of MTV China without associating it with Beijing-born Li Yifei, the channel's prominent managing director and one of *Fortune's* 25 global rising business stars in 2001. One of her achievements as a 13-year-old girl was winning the national martial arts championship for Rainbow Sword. She even played a role in China's first martial arts movie produced after the end of the 10-year Cultural Revolution, from 1966 to 1976. As a teenager, she attended the city's most elite diplomacy school, from which she graduated in 1985. Later, she went to Baylor University in the United States to study political science, which she followed with a prestigious two-month internship with the United Nations. By that time, she had lived in the United States for almost 10 years. Deciding that her future didn't lie in diplomacy, she returned to Beijing to work as a publicist for a public relations company. During that time, she worked on an account for News Corp., Viacom's rival, at which time Viacom began to take notice of her. In 1995, Li was invited to join MTV, and Sumner Redstone named her head of China's operations. Redstone apparently chose Li for three qualities: her character, her competence, and her firm commitment. Li believes that there is one more reason, and that is because she is Chinese. Her background of having lived and worked in the United States has been an additional advantage in working for MTV China.

Li typifies the generation that is coming into commercial power in the 21st century, coined as a "transitional" generation. They are the sons and daughters of the Cultural Revolution, and they will be the ones to complete China's re-emergence into the world. They think and feel like their parents, and are quite traditional and conservative; but on the other hand, they also identify with their younger counterparts. Li Yifei says of this generation, "We are living our parents' dreams." Her mother's parents were both killed during the Cultural Revolution, and it was her parents' generation who brought some measure of normalcy and stability back into the country. It is Deng Xiaoping's China that this generation is inheriting, not Mao's.

What motivates Li's generation is the desire to drive change in the right direction for the Chinese nation. A lot of her peers are internationals; Chinese nationals who have worked overseas and returned to China. Having been exposed to international and global ideas, they tend to hold key positions in the business community, which has become a lot more political. An example is Edward Tian, a graduate of Texas Tech University, who was formerly CEO of China Netcom and chairman of the Chinese equivalent of the US Federal Communications Commission.

Local Programming

MTV is continuing to roll out more local content. Li Yifei feels that her job is to be a kind of "matchmaker" between the cultures of East and West. Li prefers to bring about change by taking the middle road—she feels that she understands the Chinese culture and its systems, as well as other parts of the world and how they think and operate. She is an asset to MTV—she is straightforward, smart, and confident—despite her gender being seen as a disadvantage in China's male-dominant culture. Instead of being stymied by "roadblocks," she is able to make headway for MTV in China.

In 2001, she managed to persuade CCTV to co-produce and air China's version of the MTV Video Music Awards, the CCTV–MTV Music Honors.

CCTV–MTV Music Honors started in 1999 and is an annual ceremony that recognizes Chinese and international artists who have made a significant contribution to the global, Asian, and Chinese music industry. The first awards show had a 7.9% rating, which translated to 150 million viewers, more than half the population of the United States.

As a result of Li's powers of persuasion and communication skills, MTV has successfully acquired "landing rights" in the very modern and prosperous, thriving province of Guangdong. A deal was agreed with CCTV which saw Viacom help CCTV distribute its Channel 9 to luxury hotels in 10 major US cities, with the aim of promoting Chinese culture to the United States.

The annual *MTV Style Gala*, which made its debut in 2003, is another role model of success. It gathers together veteran singers, well-known actors, and talented artists from home and abroad, and is now one of the most-watched fashion and style shows in China. The show includes success stories from China's music, movie, and fashion industries. It is televised on MTV China's 24-hour channel and MTV's syndicated programs, as well as on Shanghai's OTV and CCTV's channel CCTV6. Other popular programs include *MTV Chart Countdown* and *MTV Music Wire*.

Strategic Partnerships

MTV is pursuing its brand journey in China with selective co-branding via strategic partnerships, two of which—those with Baidu.com and Huiyuan Juice—are particularly worthy of note.

In October 2006, MTV Networks announced a major content and advertising partnership with Baidu.com, China's number one search engine. At the time of the announcement, it was expected that the alliance agreement would give 123 million Internet users easy access to 15,000 hours of MTV and Nickelodeon original video content and music videos licensed by five top Chinese and Asian music companies for online viewing or downloading at www.baidu.com. The agreement provided for the first-ever branded area on Baidu, called *MTV Zone*, which included advertising by other global brand names such as Motorola and P&G.

The Beijing announcement also proclaimed that, because of the agreement, MTV Network's China digital media position would be extended. MTV already had at the time 100% reach to China's mobile subscribers via partnerships with China Mobile and China Unicom.

The second major partnership under the leadership of Li Yifei was that with Huiyuan Juice, China's biggest fruit juice manufacturer, announced in January 2007. The two brands are to be partners on-air and on-the-ground, the high spot placing Huiyuan Juice as the first sponsor of the 2007 *MTV Style Gala*, held in Shanghai. This is definitely a win-win situation. Huiyuan Juice gets to enhance its image on-air and further penetrate the huge youth market, while MTV gets all its Chinese events sponsored.

As Li said:

> MTV is a trendsetter and music expert with immense influence on young adults because we know what they want. Both MTV and Huiyuan are two very popular brands among youth in China. Together with Huiyuan, we are confident that our partnership will bring a healthier and more entertaining lifestyle to our young audience.

Matthew Gene Mouw, vice president of Huiyuan Juice, said:

> Partnering with MTV creates a very powerful music marketing platform that brings a chic and healthy lifestyle to every young people in China. If you wish to become a style leader in 2007, get a glass of healthy Huiyuan fruit juice and tune-in to MTV channel to watch the refreshing programming they have for you!

Clearly, both partners are very happy with their association, which adds a new dimension of social responsibility to the MTV brand, with a clear message about healthy lifestyles for young people. This should make parents happy, too!

Although the Chinese market is still young, MTV's success in China to date proves that its youth have a lot in common with their counterparts in the West when it comes to popular music and youth culture. In line with the Millennials' affinity with technology worldwide, in 2005 MTV signed an agreement with Motorola to supply the first branded music service to China Mobile's 200 million cell-phone subscribers. In essence, MTV China's brand has evolved from a mere music channel toward becoming part and parcel of China's youth culture.

MTV sees China as a strategic and huge growth market.

CONCLUSION

From the above case studies it is clear that MTV has become a global brand by swiftly and carefully entering emerging markets, giving consumers what they want, and keeping the brand relevant to their constantly changing lifestyles. In fast-growing and changing markets such as India and China, this is no mean feat.

But is it enough to secure MTV's future? All markets around the world, including those discussed above, are now embracing the digital world. MTV has remained focused on traditional media to a large extent, and must now change even more to accommodate the needs of new youth consumerism.

The next and last chapter of this book looks at what MTV has done, and needs still to do, in order to stay at the top.

1   Alex Kuruvilla, On Record by Dainik Jagran, *www.agencyfaqs.com*, September 24, 2001, http://www.agencyfaqs.com/new/interviews/data/91.html.

2   Indian Market Research Bureau, "Tuning into the Indian Youth, Part 3," 2001

3   Marc Gunther, "MTV's Passage to India," *Fortune*, August 9, 2004 http://money.cnn.com/magazines/fortune/fortune_archive/2004/08/09/377904/index.htm.

4   Ibid.

5   Ratna Bhushan, "Creating Sound Content," *The Hindu Business Line*, December 11, 2003, http://www.thehindubusinessline.com/catalyst/2003/12/11/stories/2003121100130100.htm.

6   Marc Gunther, "MTV's Passage to India," *Fortune*, August 9, 2004 http://money.cnn.com/magazines/fortune/fortune_archive/2004/08/09/377904/index.htm.

7   Interview with MTV India's GM and VP creative and content, Ashish Patil, *Radioandmusic.com*, August 23, 2007, http://www.radioandmusic.com/headlines/y2k7/aug/23august/interview_mtv.php.

8   Ibid.

9   Ibid.

10 Accenture Global Convergence Forum: Plenary Session, 2006, "Bill Unplugged: The MTV Story" *www.accenture.com*, http://www.accenture.com/Global/About_Accenture/Business_Events/By_Industry/Communications/BillRoedy.htm.

11 "India's New Worldly Women," *BusinessWeek*, August 22, 2005, http://www.businessweek.com/magazine/content/05_34/b3948530.htm.

12 "A Thousand Chinese Desires Bloom," *BusinessWeek*, August 22, 2005, http://www.businessweek.com/magazine/content/05_34/b3948531.htm.

13 Ibid.

14 Clay Chandler, "Little Emperors," *Fortune*, special issue: *Inside The New China*, October 4, 2004.

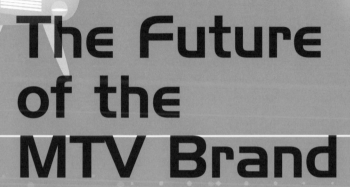

The Future
of the
MTV Brand

INTRODUCTION

What is the future of MTV? Will it survive in its present form? Will it have to transform itself given new technologies and the new revolution of the Internet? Will the Internet kill the video star?

The future of the MTV brand will depend largely on three things. First, there is the need for MTV to extend its grip on the global music television market through greater coverage in new and growing markets, keeping the balance between global and local content. Second, it must continue to understand the fast-changing needs of youth and translate these into programming content successes. Third, and this is perhaps the greatest challenge, MTV must become a dominant, if not *the* dominant, distributor of music content in the digital world.

This final chapter deals with these issues.

ESTABLISHING A PRESENCE IN NEW AND GROWING TRADITIONAL MARKETS

In the previous chapter we saw how quickly and relatively effortlessly MTV has established itself in two major and growing markets—India and China. MTV has also developed a presence in many other countries, including Russia, Pakistan, and Indonesia, with its 240 million Muslims. It is also now addressing the relatively untapped market of the Middle East.

From its base in Dubai, MTV Arabia is a 24-hour satellite channel that started broadcasting in Arabic in November 2007. Is this a risky move by MTV to try and bring an American icon to a region that has issues with Western politics? The answer is "probably not." As a frequent visitor to the Middle East, it is clear to me that youth aspirations and commonalities prevail in what is clearly a global marketplace. Go to any shopping mall and you will find young people buying Nike trainers and spending time in the big branded stores, and hanging out in Starbucks. In terms of demographics, two-thirds of the population in Arabia is aged under 25.

However, the success of MTV Arabia will rest largely on whether it can do what MTV has done in other countries in terms of localization strategy. But Bill Roedy says: "This isn't going to be MTV US... It is Arabic MTV made by Arabs for Arabs."[1] MTV is again showing that it is sensitive to local values and needs. For example, there will be an animated call to prayer every Friday at noon, Arabic productions of existing MTV shows such as *Made*, and content from India and Pakistan, from where large numbers of workers in Arabia are sourced.

The edgier and possibly offensive elements of MTV won't appear at times when families tend to watch television, and unacceptable language will be edited out, but "The idea is to encourage kids to go out and do something edgy and fun,"[2] says MTV Arabia's head of programming production, Rasha Al Emam, who is from Saudi Arabia. A typical show is *Al Hara* (meaning "The Neighborhood"). This Arabic version of *Barrio 19* will include the extreme sport of desert sand-dune driving (called "dune-bashing") and other local sports and leisure pursuits. It is estimated that approximately 40% of content will be local.

In this manner, MTV is expanding further into the global arena, but always with a global–local strategy. It excels at balancing the local element with the commonalities of global youth, but it is increasingly relying on outsourcing content to local companies in order to achieve its aims. This outsourcing of MTV's content is a bold strategy on the part of the network aimed at keeping the brand relevant and meaningful to its viewers. Once again, its irreverent approach has been amalgamated with its omnipresent relevance, resulting in the unmistakable expression of MTV's unique brand personality. MTV will likely continue to outsource content as a means of reaching a massive, growing, and increasingly complex Asian market.

CHANGES IN YOUTH COMMONALITIES AND THE MTV BRAND

MTV has a better understanding of the needs of youth than most brands, especially entertainment brands. Young people the world over have many behavioral and attitudinal commonalities that don't change as time goes by, including the desire to express their lives and personalities through music. What MTV has done well, is to anticipate and understand the commonalities that have and haven't changed, and to interpret and present them well.

The concerns of youth the world over have changed little in the past decade or so with respect to religion, war, crime, and employment. But added to these are concerns about urbanization, poverty, global warming/pollution, and HIV/AIDS. All these issues invade the lives of young people every day via all forms of media, and they take them very seriously.

Similarly, the ways in which young people like to express themselves are fairly consistent over time, though they may be manifested in different ways. Fashion, for example, has provided an outlet for "metrosexuality." But largely global commonalities remain similar as generations move on.

What has changed significantly over time is the use of media and technology in association with these commonalities of behavior and attitude, and how youth has embraced them. The advent of new innovations, especially with respect to the convergence of technologies, is the driving force behind this trend, and it is in this area where youth is gravitating toward and influencing global brand development.

The strength of the MTV brand is not only that it keeps in step with its target audience, but also that it stays just ahead of the curve in terms of viewers' trend-related twists and turns. The network's acute intuitive insight or perceptiveness—to the point of being clairvoyant—is undeniable, and is attributed to its relentless consumer-focused research. With this in mind, MTV has created four dimensions of focus for the brand's future. These are:

- media
- self-expression
- security
- technology.

Media

The focus for platforms of delivery for the MTV of the future will have to be mainly technology-driven media. This is discussed further later in this chapter, but suffice it to say here that MTV will have to have strong online and offline media strategies. As such, it will need to embrace not just the traditional delivery of TV and magazines, but also the multifaceted Internet.

Self-expression and Security

The need for youth to express itself through the media hasn't changed, as is the case with fashion. But young people today want to express their views more loudly than previous generations on worldly issues such as sexuality, drugs and alcohol, poverty, and the like. Similarly, youth is very vocal on issues of security, such as religion, war, crime, and global warming. MTV realizes that music is a powerful influence on youth and that it can evoke change. By providing a global forum for self-expression, it gives young people a means to voice their concerns.

Technology

Although the emphasis on content will reflect the changing behavioral and attitudinal commonalities of security and self-expression, content will also be delivered through the newer and growing channels, such as mobile and video games, and through the latest devices, such as iPods and others. The rapid convergence of technology will be a driver of this trend, and it is this area that poses the biggest challenge for the future of the MTV brand, as discussed below.

THE FIGHT FOR DIGITAL SPACE: MTV'S INITIAL STEPS

The real challenge for the MTV business and brand comes not so much from the more traditional areas mentioned above, but from the rise of digital and Internet technology, which is revolutionizing the world of music. It is important to analyze this challenge and MTV's response in some depth.

The Reality of Technology Convergence

The traditional boundaries between content and distribution are fast disappearing. Digital technology has been embraced most rapidly by youth, who are always on their mobile phones and enjoy moving between platforms. Connectivity is an essential part of their everyday lives. The huge opportunities arising from the digital revolution are changing at lightning speed, and only agile companies with the right kind of talent will be able to take advantage of them.

The face of entertainment is, accordingly, changing rapidly, and this poses a distinct challenge for MTV. The success of the brand to date has been due largely to a complete victory in the medium of television, as represented by the name "Music Television" and the famous initials "MTV." But we now live in a digital world, where everyone, especially youth, is looking for and finding new forms of access to entertainment and music. The fight has now moved significantly from cable television to the Internet. The winners will be those who dominate digital space, and the Internet medium that gives them access to it, in new and exciting ways. Where television is basically a one-way channel, the Internet provides consumers with two-way communications capabilities.

MTV has an apparent disadvantage here that it is attempting to rectify with large numbers of organizational and staff changes. The MTV supertanker has to change direction without losing speed, a task it acknowledges. As MTV president Christina Norman says, "MTV has a history of surrounding the consumer with both long-form and interstitial content, and I think we can deliver on a two-way relationship with our audience."[3]

How is MTV adapting strategically to the new challenges?

Convergence is Here Now

With the proliferation of broadband Internet access and the falling prices of data storage, people are beginning to put all aspects of their life into a digital format. Music, movies, video games, and television shows are already piped into their laptops, mobile phones, cars, and living rooms. There is a huge global trend away from TV to mobile centricity in particular. The annual global spend by young people is around US$106 billion, with US$16 billion of that spent on music.[4]

MTV has to enter full tilt into the new millennium and create a digitalization edge if its expansion and growth are to meet its internal and external expectations. Since the turn of the century, it seems to be doing so. From its programming, to its hiring of staff, to its content distribution throughout the world, MTV has become more fluid, efficient, and quicker to access, through the use of multimedia platforms such as the Internet (not just the normal dial-up connection, but broadband, wireless Internet connections), mobile phones (3G, 4G), and newer platforms such as Microsoft's Xbox 360. But is this enough, and is it fast enough?

Let's take a look at what has happened to date. In October 2005, MTV Networks and Microsoft announced a joint effort, based on Microsoft Windows XP Media Center Edition 2005 and the Xbox 360 game console, that will see users able to switch seamlessly between a standard TV experience and on-demand broadband programming without ever leaving the couch—in other words, integrated digital entertainment for the home.

There is no doubt that TV has become a large part of people's lives, and that mobile subscriptions in some countries have reached a saturated level, notable exceptions being China and India. The result is that convergence of technology for TV and mobile has become an organic process, with interactive TV as an extension for advertising purposes. Therefore, it has come as no surprise that MTV has taken advantage of this, crafting content such as *Head and Body* "mobisodes" (mobile + episodes) for mobile TV users.

The technology market research firm In-Stat estimates that with the emerging availability of mobile TV, whether it be a mobile video phone or a broadcast TV handset, the number of mobile TV users will increase from 1.1 million worldwide in 2005[5] to over 124.8 million by 2010.[6] The driver of all the trends mentioned is that each person wants his or her own individual choices to be instantly available.

Mass Individualized Customization

MTV has responded to the mobile challenge and now airs some of its shows first on mobile, then on TV. Also, with its acquisition of online video company iFilm, MTV can now distribute huge numbers of videos to mobile users. iFilm is now part of the SPIKE website. In fact, MTV has over 63 partnerships globally[7] with mobile operators to deliver digital content, and the capability to deliver video games to mobile with its Game One offering. The result is that MTV is rapidly moving into the business of mass customization.

A new benefit for all sides—whether it is MTV, or the advertisers, or the consumers—is that technology has fueled the possibility of not just mass customization, but individual customization. The technologically savvy are now able to download anything that interests them, and edit it to eliminate what they don't want, thus setting their own "play list" and, now, "video list" as seen implemented on MTV's broadband channel, MTV Overdrive. Furthermore, they are able to interact directly with MTV in order to get what they want.

A fascinating aspect of this trend is the ability to access digital entertainment anywhere the user wants it. It is no wonder that the age of digitalization has pushed the brand forward by further enhancing MTV's slogan: "I want my MTV!"

The intangible personal deliverables the viewer receives, whether it is hearing the kind of music they like, or finding and interacting with others with similar tastes, translate to personal empowerment. The convergence of music and technology provides the viewer with a unique connection to music and inventiveness.

MTV Gets the URGE

The URGE digital music service was launched jointly by MTV Networks and Microsoft in early 2007. This new music store initiative competes to some degree with iTunes from Apple (it cannot be used to download music to iPods), and with Napster, Yahoo!, and RealNetworks' Rhapsody.

Unlike iTunes, URGE is a fee-based subscription service that allows people to listen to vast amounts of music via the Microsoft Windows Media Player 11 beta software, although other online music stores can be browsed through Windows software without installation of URGE. In addition, URGE allows viewers to visit MTV, VH1, or other pages, and to create custom play lists. MTV videos are also available, but URGE is still in its infancy and much more development work is needed. As of March 2007, it was only reachable in the United States and in US territories and possessions. In August 2007, URGE was merged with Rhapsody and its life as a separate music service came to an end.

Providing People Power—Competitive Landscape

During the past three decades, the MTV brand has more than proved its capability to endure and to reinvent itself, but the advent of new media typified by providers such as News Corp.'s MySpace and Google's YouTube has caused management to rethink the brand's future. People today want more power and control over what they do online, and who they do it with. For example, anyone can now go online and discuss and share videos and other information about themselves, but the music business model has changed. For instance, traditionally a music band would need to get a contract with a music label, get airtime on radio, and hopefully take off with plays on the best TV channel in the world—MTV. Now, a band can go from nowhere to the top without taking any of these intermediary steps, simply by posting video footage of itself on the Internet.

YouTube and MySpace have taken an outright lead in giving online youth what they want. For example, MySpace.com users use the site to make friends, do professional networking, and for dating and sharing interests. In 2005, Rupert Murdoch's News Corp. bought Intermix Media, owner of MySpace.com, the fifth most viewed Internet domain in the United States and owner of other sites, for US$580 million. News Corp. announced that it expected the networking site would drive traffic to Murdoch's Fox TV sites.

Are Digital Players Moving MTV Down the Value Chain?

MySpace has injected a lot of pace into the digital music race. As a very successful social network, it is now set to offer what many observers see as an Internet version of MTV's *Unplugged*; called *Transmissions*, musicians are invited to choose a studio location in which to perform the songs they want to record. MySpace then shows and offers for sale the videos of the artists' performances. The difference between this and the traditional *Unplugged* is that MySpace gets revenue immediately, whereas *Unplugged* released its products months after the event.

MySpace also offers instant gratification to consumers, as downloads are available immediately. The advantage to the artists is that they can choose their distribution channel. The first singer to appear was James Blunt, who was impressed by the flexibility of the process. "Through MySpace," he said, "I can get songs heard that are any length I choose, that are any format I choose."[8] This kind of competitive move puts a great deal of pressure on MTV to stay in touch with consumer trends. For example, in October 2007, MySpace became the third-largest music website with 17.9 million unique visitors, behind Yahoo Music with 22.4 million and ArtistDirect with 19.1 million. But the MySpace website enjoyed a 42% increase in traffic, year on year, making it the fastest-growing site.[9]

If artists are looking at new channels as a means of breaking into the music elite, MTV is in danger of being moved down the value chain. Another example of how digital Internet competitors are repositioning MTV can be seen in the rise to stardom of singer Colbie Caillat, a 22-year-old from California. Caillat "made it" on MySpace in 2007 after some friends uploaded her music. As a result of her almost instant fame (three million visits and 10 million plays), she was signed by Universal Music. Only subsequently did she appear on MTV and VH1, followed by recordings made at the famous Abbey Road Studios in London.

Furthermore, if we look more broadly at competitive challenges, we should not overlook the possibility that global innovators in music and communication (for example, Apple) might try to make a move into mobile video music content. Such a move would be a serious threat to any player, including MTV.

The speed of growth of these new digital channels that give youth freedom, self-expression, and instant music gratification will continue exponentially in coming years. In truth, MTV has been a little slow in adapting to the above changes, but it is now moving rapidly to address this critical brand management issue.

One response from MTV's parent Viacom was to ask YouTube[10] to remove thousands of video clips derived from Viacom's programming. Content from MTV, along with other channels such as Comedy Central, Nickelodeon, VH1, CMT, SPIKE, and BET, was included in a takedown demand of around 160,000 clips. Negotiations broke down on the issue of sharing of revenues, and because Google didn't remove content as quickly as Viacom wanted. As a result, in March 2007, a US$1 billion lawsuit was issued by Viacom for copyright infringement by YouTube. The outcome of this case is unlikely to be revealed before this book goes to print.

A more interesting and forward-looking business initiative was to develop a strategic partnership with Joost (pronounced "Juiced"), the Internet video service under development by the founders of Skype. Launched as a *beta* version in October 2007, this Internet video platform will enable much Viacom-owned "television and theatrical programming" to be viewed, such as MTV's *Real World, Punk'd, Laguna Beach,* and *Beavis & Butt-Head.* Viewers will be able to watch Viacom content free of charge, and to engage in Web discussion, social networking, annotation, and community features.

Phillipe Dauman, Viacom president and CEO, said: "We're extremely pleased to be working with Joost, and couldn't be prouder to be a key partner in the launch of the next generation in broadband video technology." He added:

> We're determined to keep pushing and growing our digital presence and bring our programming to audiences on every platform and device that they want... [W]e will continue to seek out partners like Joost, which has created an exciting breakthrough platform that represents not only a fantastic user experience, but one that is built on a compelling and sustainable business model that respects both content creators and consumers.

In addition to Joost, Viacom has established agreements with Warner Music Group and production company Endemol.[11]

There is absolutely no doubt that, if it is to survive, MTV must become a major player in the digital and Internet space, and it seems determined to do so. Responding with technological advances is one thing; however, to be really effective, MTV must understand the changing needs and wants of its customers with respect to interactive content.

As part of the evolution of the MTV brand, changes have been made to its tangible functions such as programming and distribution, as well as to the intangible values of the brand itself. Great brands continuously evolve in order to stay modern and relevant to their target audiences, and MTV is no exception.

ADJUSTMENT OF BRAND VALUES

Along with the changes in its business strategy outlined in this chapter, MTV has also adjusted its core values, although its brand personality characteristics largely remain intact. In 2005, it adjusted its values to those shown below:[12]

- **Status:** value in being a youth-minded, forward-thinking person whether 13 or 49, optimistic.

- **Irreverent approach:** continuously challenging *ways it's always been done,* "respect" vs. "one size fits all."

- **Omnipresent relevance:** on-the-go, lifestyle-ready, experience-obsessed, beyond "novelty" to "necessity."

- **Connective/personal discovery:** participatory, sense of ownership, ability to create and produce.

- **Extraordinary:** via seamless connection to media powerhouse of MTV proper, access, abundance of selection, share-worthy.

- **Exclusive:** unique sensibility and packaging, content, "feels like the right fit here."

- **Concierge-like:** smart; recognize the *consumer in you,* "celebration of intelligence" vs. "just confident."

CONCLUSION: WILL THE INTERNET KILL THE VIDEO STAR?

There is no doubting that the MTV brand has become one of the world's most powerful brands, and that this power hasn't come about by accident. MTV has dominated the world of music television, and has stayed relevant to the needs and wants of youth, since its inception. The basic concerns of youth, and the need for young people to express views on these areas of concern, haven't fundamentally changed in that time, but the ways in which young people adopt new ways of living their lives do change and so youth-focused brands have to stay relevant and empathetic to their market.

Until just the last couple of years, MTV has met these challenges. However, with the growing popularity of the Internet as a music channel, and as technology becomes more sophisticated, allowing access to mobile music and video content, MTV is in danger of becoming "un-cool." It certainly hasn't pioneered this trend, and so it must move more quickly to keep up with the pace. Yahoo!, MySpace, and YouTube are embarking on the same strategy and competing for the same audience as MTV, but they are striking more deals to broadcast music videos via broadband. In doing so, they are eating into MTV's market share, and there is no room for complacency on MTV's part.

MTV is hitting back by acquiring the gaming sites Xfire.com and Game Trailers and the film site iFilm.com, but it failed to buy MySpace, losing out to News Corp. If it is to compete fully, it will have to acquire or partner with more music and film sites, and it must get a decent share of the social networking arena.

Although the rush is on, MTV certainly is neither panicking nor lacking in confidence and understands the need to reinvent itself. CEO of MTV Networks Judy McGrath is making sure that services are delivered across the range of new channels, including broadband, mobile phones and games, and says, "Nobody wants to be who they used to be and that includes us", whilst insisting that "we're more inside the heads of our audience than anybody else." President and chief operating officer Michael J. Wolff adds, "The Internet is no longer about text. It's about video. We produce and own more video than anybody."[13]

In the final analysis, MTV should be seen as an integral part of parent Viacom's digital strategy. MTV Networks knows more about youth than any other entertainment company, and it is unlikely to run for second place. Given that it will compete fiercely in the growing phenomenon of digital space, the aura and equity of the brand means that MTV will still be the premier brand to go to for music artists and music lovers. The Internet won't kill the video star; indeed, it may well make it stronger.

[1] Kerry Capell, "The Arab World Wants Its MTV," *BusinessWeek*, October 11, 2007, http://www.businessweek.com/globalbiz/content/oct2007/gb20071011_342851.htm.

[2] Ibid.

[3] David Carr, "Do They Still Want Their MTV? A Changing Format," *International Herald Tribune*, February 19, 2007, http://www.iht.com/articles/2007/02/19/yourmoney/mtv.php.

[4] Accenture Global Convergence Forum: Plenary Session, 2006, "Bill Unplugged: The MTV Story." *www.accenture.com*, http://www.accenture.com/Global/About_Accenture/Business_Events/By_Industry/Communications/BillRoady.htm.

[5] "Mobile Video is a Tough Sell According to In-Stat," In-Stat Press Releases, July 18, 2005, http://www.in-stat.com/press.asp?ID=1407&sku=IN0502050MCD.

[6] "124.8 Million Broadcast Mobile TV Users Worldwide by 2010," *www.3gnewsroom.com*, April 30, 2005, http://www.3gnewsroom.com/3g_news/apr_05/news_5811.shtml.

[7] Eric Sylvers, "MTV Comes to Small Screen for T-Mobile Users," *International Herald Tribune*, March 8, 2006, http://www.iht.com/articles/2006/03/07/yourmoney/mtv.php.

[8] "MySpace Set to Show and Sell Music Videos," *International Herald Tribune,* December 5, 2007.

[9] Ibid.

[10] Anne Broache and Greg Sandoval, "Viacom Sues Google over YouTube Clips," *CNET.news.com,* March 13, 2007, http://www.news.com/Viacom-sues-Google-over-YouTube-clips/2100-1030_3-6166668.html?tag=cd.hed.

[11] Andrew Orlowski, "Joost–the New, New TV Thing," *The Register,* January 17, 2007, http://www.theregister.co.uk/2007/01/17/joost/.

[12] Reproduced with permission of MTV Networks International.

[13] Tom Lowry, "Can MTV Stay Cool?" *BusinessWeek,* February 20, 2006, http://www.businessweek.com/magazine/content/06_08/b3972001.htm